THE MAKING OF A CHRISTIAN

CHARLES DAVIS

THE MAKING OF A CHRISTIAN

Five Lectures on Christian Initiation

SHEED AND WARD

LONDON AND NEW YORK

FIRST PUBLISHED 1964
SHEED AND WARD LTD
33 MAIDEN LANE
LONDON W.C.2
AND
SHEED AND WARD INC
64 UNIVERSITY PLACE
NEW YORK 3

NIHIL OBSTAT: JOANNES M. T. BARTON, S.T.D., L.S.S.
  CENSOR DEPUTATUS

IMPRIMATUR: ✠ GEORGIUS L. CRAVEN,
  EPUS SEBASTAPOLIS VIC. GEN.

WESTMONASTERII, DIE 5A NOV. 1963

The *Nihil Obstat* and *Imprimatur* are a declaration that a book
or pamphlet is considered to be free from doctrinal or moral
error. It is not implied that those who have granted the *Nihil
Obstat* or *Imprimatur* agree with the contents, opinions or statements expressed.

This book is set in 11 pt. Linotype Baskerville

*Made and printed in Great Britain by
William Clowes and Sons, Limited, London and Beccles*

CONTENTS

chapter		page
1.	SYMBOL AND PROMISE	1
2.	THE CHURCH AND HER RITES	37
3.	DEATH AND RESURRECTION	76
4.	ANOINTED WITH THE SPIRIT	115
5.	WITNESSES OF CHRIST	144

SYMBOL AND PROMISE

MANY people think that the metaphor of washing sums up all the teaching on baptism. The purpose of this sacrament, they will immediately answer, is to cleanse us from original sin and so its outward sign is a bodily wash, done to symbolize the spiritual washing of the soul. It is a pity that so impoverished a view is widespread. Not merely does it fail to do justice to the purpose and effects of the sacrament, but it also gives a most inadequate account of its symbolism. The metaphor of washing is scriptural, and it is also of long usage in other religions. But in either case it is but one feature in a much richer imagery. We have badly overworked a single element in baptismal symbolism, while neglecting the rest.

Think how unlike a wash baptism really is. A wash is not an exciting event; even the voluptuous would not call a bath thrilling—or would they? Well, at any rate they would not put it in the same class of events as a birth. But baptism is the emergence of new life and should provoke the same wonder as a birth. Again, a wash is superficial; it does not penetrate within or change what we are. But baptism changes a man through and through; it profoundly alters him and affects his personality. Finally, we must wash ourselves frequently; the need continually recurs: baptism cannot be repeated; it is as definitive as creation. Clearly, we are not going to get very far in understanding baptism if we are content to think of it as a washing of the soul.

Why, then, use water? Does not the popular, feeble understanding of baptism come from the fact that we do baptize by the gesture of washing? No; the action of baptizing is not just a gesture of washing; it has a much greater symbolic value than that. People are missing the full meaning that water has when used symbolically.

There are two reasons for the lack of understanding. The first is the way the sacrament is now carried out. The main sacramental action has been reduced to a minimal gesture: instead of a pool and immersion, we have a font and a trickle of water. The stress on what is required for validity and on the objective efficacy of that part has led to a neglect of all the other elements that make up the full sacramental sign. More often than not these are hurried over without the deliberate care necessary if a symbol is to affect the mind and if people are to take part profitably in symbolic actions. Since these secondary rites are intended to deepen the impression given by the main action, which they lead up to and follow, the impact of the chief symbol is seriously weakened by neglecting them. But until quite recently the principal barrier to understanding was the use of a language unintelligible to nearly all the faithful. Words are indispensable to developed symbolism. At its best, an action by itself does not tell us much about the reality it represents; to exist fully as a symbol it must be completed by words. Unintelligible words and hurried gestures make it impossible for a symbol to act upon the mind. People ought to have grown in their understanding of baptism by taking part frequently in its celebration as parents and godparents or simply as members of the Christian community; instead, its celebration has been largely meaningless to them, and they have drawn their knowledge of the meaning of baptism from the thin theological statement in the catechism, not from the rich symbolism of the rite. It may be added that the Easter Vigil, particularly the consecration of the font, is an integral part of the sacramental sign of baptism, necessary for a proper grasp of the Church's understanding of this sacrament. Only in recent years has this paschal celebration been brought once more to the attention of the average Catholic. Certainly, then, one of the reasons for the general lack of understanding is the way baptism has usually been celebrated.

But there is a second reason, and this can prevent understanding even when the first has been counteracted. Why is it that some people remain unmoved, out of touch with what is going on, despite a careful and intelligent celebration of baptism and a giving of due prominence to the Easter Vigil? The reason, I suggest, is a gap in their mental outlook, caused by ignorance of the Bible. Where a community expresses its belief and worship in developed symbols, as Christians do in the sacraments, this presupposes a common mentality. And a common mentality demands a common fund of words, a common memory of past great events and a common store of images and themes. Without such a common mentality, symbolic communication, other than the crudest, is simply not feasible. Have Christians as a body such a common mentality? In theory, yes. The mentality that is supposedly ours, that must be ours if we are to take part intelligently in the sacraments, is that found in the Bible. The Bible—read by the Church, of course—gives us our common spiritual culture. It is the record of our history; in it we find the images and themes that we share together like common property.

The Bible provides what we need for a common consciousness. So, the second reason why people miss the full meaning of the baptismal symbol is ignorance of its biblical context. Many are unfamiliar with what should be, as it were, their native language and culture as Christians. Isolated symbols without the resonance in the mind given by multiple association have little impact. Can we, then, expect the sacraments to mean much when the Bible is known little?

Since the meaning of a sacrament is expressed in the symbols it uses, the first task in studying a sacrament is to examine these in the light of their biblical context. Baptism has gathered to itself a rich cluster of images from the Bible. But before I begin to take this cluster apart a preliminary question must be settled. Can the symbolism of one culture, in this case the Semitic culture, remain valid and effective for men, like ourselves, who live in an entirely different culture? It sounds all right at first, it may be objected, to say that we must acquire a common mentality by reading the Bible, but this is simply not practicable. Conditions of life are so different for us from what they were for the Hebrews that it is unnatural to us to use their symbols. We may learn to recognize and manipulate them, but they can never mean much to us as symbols. So the objection runs on, until we

remember that God has made the Bible the
permanent vehicle of his revelation, the permanent expression of his message. It is for all ages
the Word of God. We must indeed transpose its
teaching into other terms to meet fresh problems, to draw out its meaning, to relate it to
advances in human thought and to present it in
a language they understand to men who would
otherwise find it unintelligible. But for Christians within the Church, the Bible as it stands,
with its own themes and images, remains the
privileged expression of their faith, the raw
material, as it were, of the Church's prayer and
the source of her sacramental symbolism.

Yet, there is some force in the objection. God
could not have given the Bible the place it
occupies, unless he had providentially adapted
it to its purpose. The Bible must have qualities
that make it possible to insert it into all human
cultures. To develop this point fully is not to
our present purpose, but one feature of the
Bible's perennial appeal is very relevant here:
the Bible uses and develops the basic human
symbols common to men of all times. By basic
human symbols I mean what Jung calls primordial or archetypal images: the coming into
consciousness as images or symbols of the arche-
types or contents of that collective unconscious
which is part of the fabric of the psyche. These

are images that keep recurring in one form or other in religions, myths, folklore and poetry. The Bible handles these images in a way proper to itself and, in particular, gives them what they lack elsewhere, an historical reference to actual events. But it is all the time moulding to its own special purpose a symbolism that corresponds to the deep recesses of the human mind.

This is especially true of water, the chief baptismal symbol. In mythology and, if we believe the psychologists, in the depths of our individual minds, water always has a double meaning: it is at one and the same time the symbol of death and of life. Water is the element of death. It represents the forces of dissolution and disintegration. The enemy of this world of order and form, it is the hostile power that strives to reduce all once more to formless chaos. To go down into water is to enter darkness and death; it is to be submerged in a sea where all is dissolved. Yet, water is the source of life. In accounts of the origin of the world, including that of the Bible, water is seen as the mother-element from which all things came forth. This maternal meaning of water is applied to individual men by calling "water" the fluid that surrounds the child in the womb. And water is not only at the origin of life, it is also the means of its renewal. Water dissolves in order to purify and renew. To pass through water is to be reinvigorated, to find new youth and fresh vigour. In the depths of water lies hidden the secret of regeneration.

Lying behind the developed themes of the Bible is this primitive twofold meaning of water. It comes to expression in the opening verses of the Book of Genesis. "God, at the beginning of time, created heaven and earth. Earth was still an empty waste, and darkness hung over the deep; but already, over its waters, stirred the breath of God." (Gen. 1.1-2.)[1] Water here is the primeval chaos, and from one point of view it is a hostile element that recedes before the word of God as it creates distinction and order. But from another point of view it is the womb of all things, made fruitful by the spirit or breath of God with which it is associated.

For the Hebrews, then, water meant death and destruction. As a people they detested and feared the sea, which for them represented primitive chaos by its turbulence. "All about me surged the waves of death", we read in Psalm 17, "deep flowed the perilous tide, to daunt me; the grave had caught me in its toils, deadly snares had trapped my feet." And again in Psalm 68: "Save me from sinking in the mire, rescue me

---

[1] Scripture quotations are from the Knox version, unless otherwise indicated.

from my enemies, from the deep waters that surround me; let me not sink under the flood, swallowed up in its depths, and the well's mouth close above me." Water is an enemy, a cause of distress and death; man must be rescued from it by God. "Out of the depths I cry to thee, O Lord", is the opening of the familiar Psalm 129. When the Apocalypse describes the new heaven and the new earth, it notes, "and there was no more sea." (Apoc. 21.1.)

But water meant life also. This is not surprising in a people formed in the desert and living in a land where water was still scarce and manifestly the cause of life. The story is told of an Arab who crossed the Mediterranean to France and there came upon a waterfall. He stood gazing at it for some time and then turned to a person near by and said, "Does it never stop?" The symbolism universally associated with water was reinforced in the lands of the Bible by the fact that water was precious through scarcity.

Right through the Bible we have the theme of water as bringing life. Genesis tells us how the rivers of Paradise made it a garden of delight —a point taken up in the blessing of the font, when the priest says as he divides the water with his hand, ". . . who caused thee to flow from a well in paradise and bade thee water the whole

earth in four streams".[1] In the heavenly city of
the Apocalypse there is "a river, whose waters
give life; it flows, clear as crystal, from the throne
of God, from the throne of the Lamb". (Apoc.
22.1.) The Psalmist sings of the Lord his shepherd, "He gives me a resting-place where there is
green pasture, leads me out to the cool water's
brink, refreshed and content." (Ps. 22.) Another
psalm, Psalm 41, begins, "O God, my whole soul
longs for thee, as a deer for running water; my
whole soul thirsts for God, the living God." This
psalm was sung by the candidates for baptism
as on Easter Night they made their way in procession to the baptistery. It is still sung when the
baptismal water, after its blessing, is carried to
the font. We again find the theme of water as
giving life when the prophet gives this promise
from God to the people in exile: "I will pour
out water on the thirsty plain, streams over the
land that once was dry; I will pour out my spirit
upon thy race, my blessing on all thy line, and
where the grass springs up they shall spring up
too, like willows by running water." (Isa. 44.3–4.)

Christ took up this familiar theme when he
told the Samaritan woman he would give men

[1] The translation of passages from the Holy Week
rites is taken from *The Missal in Latin and English*,
prepared by The Very Rev. J. B. O'Connell and
H. P. R. Finberg. (Burns Oates & Washbourne,
London.)

living water to bring them everlasting life. The passage in John that recounts this (John 4.5–42) was used in the preparation of catechumens for baptism; it was the Gospel of one of the masses connected with the scrutinies. A little further on in John's Gospel we are told how on the Feast of Tabernacles one year Christ stood in the Temple and cried aloud, "If any man is thirsty, let him come to me, and drink." (John 7.37.) The text goes on to speak of fountains of living water, and John explains that this water is the Spirit coming to us from the risen Christ. It had not yet been given, he says, because Christ had not yet been raised to glory.

We seem to have passed from the theme of water to that of the Spirit, but actually the merging of the two themes is biblical. It is not surprising that the two should have come together. Water is a source of life and the Spirit is too, and so water came to symbolize the Spirit. The biblical teaching on the Spirit evolved from two primitive ideas: the breath of life in man that was seen as something divine, and the winds coming from the world above as messengers of God and instruments of his purpose. If the winds came from the west, they brought rain and life and were signs of his favour, if they came from the east they brought burning heat and death and were signs of his anger. These two ideas, the

breath of the living and the winds, were gradually "spiritualized", and there developed the
complex notion of the Spirit of God, the breath
of God and his vehement power, acting in the
world, given to the prophets and other leaders
in Israel, with an outpouring on all men
promised for messianic times. Like the rain-
bearing winds, the Spirit of God brought life.
So the giving of the Spirit was described as a
downpour of rain on the desert, or the flowing
of abundant streams renewing the face of the
earth. With Christ came the further revelation
of the Holy Spirit as a divine person; and the
universal outpouring of the Spirit promised to
men comes from the risen Christ. We come
under this in the waters of baptism, which are
thus the symbol of the Spirit.

But we are moving ahead too quickly. Let us
retrace our steps. Water for the Hebrews was
both an enemy, symbolizing death and destruction, and a source of life, in which role it was
associated with the Spirit. Now, this double
meaning of water is presupposed in the accounts
given in the Old Testament of various episodes
in sacred history. Sacred history consists of events
that were seen by faith as saving actions of God.
God has intervened in this world on behalf of
his chosen people and, as was gradually understood, for the salvation of the human race as a

whole. Before Christ, the greatest of the events that were embodiments of the divine saving power was the Exodus or the rescue of the Israelites from Egypt. It was to this and to the other events of sacred history that the Apostles and the early Church turned when in their teaching they tried to explain the reality they had themselves experienced in the risen Christ and in the descent of the Spirit upon them at Pentecost, a reality that was communicated to their converts by baptism and the other sacraments. They explained this new Christian reality by calling upon the Old Testament; they expressed it in terms of what God had already done.

What lies behind this appeal to the Old Testament is a conviction of the unity and continuity of God's plan and the insight that God's saving activity followed a fundamentally identical pattern in both Old and New Testaments. God in fact has always been doing the same thing, though with ever greater and deeper effect as the history of salvation advanced to its climax in Christ. To discern the meaning of the new Christian thing we have at hand the story of what God did for his people. Now possessing the Spirit, we can there perceive the pattern and purpose of God's work of love, which forms a single whole. This is the method that was begun in the New Testament itself, continued in the catechetical instructions of the Fathers and is still found in the Liturgy. To follow it means to explain baptism by seeking types of baptism in the Old Testament. But these types are not mere illustrations or pictorial aids for Christian children; they are divine actions that were genuine anticipations of baptism, revealing already the pattern of the divine reality it embodies. They prepared the way for baptism, and there is a real continuity between them and baptism, in which God completes what he began in the Old Testament.

The awareness of an identity of pattern between one stage in the history of salvation and the next led to the application of the same procedure to the incidents of Christ's earthly life. The actions of Christ during his public ministry are seen as foreshadowing the actions of the risen Christ in the Church through the sacraments. This is already done in the Gospel of St. John. He sees the miracles of Christ as symbolic of the sacraments, so that his presentation of the life of Christ contains a rich sacramental theology. This has been used by the Liturgy.

One further remark before I examine the types of baptism more closely. Water, with its double meaning, is central in baptismal typology, but it is not the only element. Other features in the events seen as types are given a symbolic value. This happens, for example, with many incidents in the Exodus story. Some of the analogies drawn may seem far-fetched; some are indeed far-fetched. But however forced may be some of the elements in these groups of symbols, the insight that provoked the working out of such details was sound: the events chosen as types really contained the divine action and gift of baptism in a preparatory anticipation.

The first of the four readings that open the baptismal part of the Easter Vigil is the narrative of creation from the Book of Genesis. This gives us our first type of baptism: creation.

To understand creation as a baptismal type we must first get used to the idea that for the Israelites creation belonged to the category of saving events. They did not start with the doctrine of creation, as we so often do, and make the covenant of God with his people subordinate to it. They started with the Covenant and saw creation as its necessary condition, as the opening action that led to it. God had the Covenant in view when he created. Creation is the way to the Covenant, and the Covenant is the goal of creation. The work of creation is the beginning of the history of salvation; it is the prologue to the story of God's dealings with mankind. This understanding of creation as a saving event made it natural for the Israelites to conceive the messianic salvation they awaited in hope as a new and more wonderful creation. The first creation became the figure of the new creation to come. (See Isa. 65. 17–25.)

The New Testament shows us the work of Christ as being the new creation. Baptism is its personal accomplishment in each individual. So St. Paul writes, "When a man becomes a new creature in Christ, his old life has disappeared" (2 Cor. 5.17); and again, "Circumcision means nothing, the want of it means nothing; when a man is in Christ Jesus, there has been a new creation." (Gal. 6.15.) And Paul is still thinking of baptism when he says, "God has created us in Christ Jesus, pledged to such good actions as he has prepared beforehand, to be the employment of our lives." (Eph. 2.10.) It is the same theme that is in question when baptism is described as a rebirth in Christ's discourse to Nicodemus. Already in Matthew's Gospel the coming of the new order had been called a new birth: "Jesus said to them, I promise you, in the new birth, when the Son of Man sits on the throne of his glory, you also shall sit there on twelve thrones" (Matt. 19.28); the passage in John uses the idea to declare the meaning of baptism. "Jesus answered, Believe me, no man can enter into the kingdom of God unless birth

comes to him from water, and from the Holy
Spirit. What is born by natural birth is a thing
of nature, what is born by spiritual birth is a
thing of spirit. Do not be surprised, then, at my
telling thee, You must be born anew." (John
3.5–7.)

The mention of water brings us back to the
first creation as the type of the second. The
primeval waters foreshadow the waters of baptism. We have already seen their double role
and their association with the Spirit. The same
applies to the waters of baptism. When we enter
them our old life disappears and what we are is
dissolved, but born in the waters by the Spirit
we come out as new men to a new existence.
Christian tradition stresses also that this rebirth
from water takes place at the summons of God's
word. The action of the word in the sacraments
is compared to the part attributed to God's word
in the account of the first creation.

One action in God's work of creation was felt
as having a particular significance: the creation
of light. "Then God said, Let there be light;
and the light began. God saw the light, and
found it good, and he divided the spheres of
light and darkness." (Gen. 1.3–4.) The contrast
between darkness and light lends itself to development, and, as we all know, it was in fact
used to express the significance of Christ's work.

That Christ is "the true light" that enlightens every man is stated in the prologue of John's Gospel, and it forms one of the major themes of that Gospel. Its application to baptism is not surprising.

In the account of the cure of the man born blind (John 9.1–41) we have an excellent example of how John interprets the miracles of Christ as containing teaching about the sacraments. This miracle is taken as a figure of baptism. John relates that Christ spread clay on the man's eyes and said, "I am the world's light." Then he sent him to the pool of Siloe to wash. The name actually means "conduit", but John for his own purpose takes it as meaning "Sent" —that is, Christ. What he is telling his readers is that in this command to wash in a pool that bears Christ's name he saw an action that prophetically signified baptism. Thus, Christ's reference to himself as the light of the world is explained: he illuminates us, opens our eyes, in the waters of baptism. As we might expect, the Church made use of this passage in her baptismal liturgy; it is the Gospel text of one of the masses for the scrutinies.

That baptism is an illumination is confirmed by other texts from the New Testament. St. Paul makes a reference to the first creation when he writes: "The same God who bade light shine out of darkness has kindled a light in our hearts, whose shining is to make known his glory as he has revealed it in the features of Jesus Christ." (2 Cor. 4.6.) The underlying reference to baptism is clearer in this text from Colossians: "Thanking God our Father for making us fit to share the light which saints inherit, for rescuing us from the power of darkness, and transferring us to the kingdom of his beloved Son." (Col. 1.12–13.) In the Epistle to the Ephesians we have a verse that is probably taken from an early baptismal hymn: "Awake, thou that sleepest, and arise from the dead, and Christ shall give thee light." (Eph. 5.14.) Paul has just said: "Once you were all darkness; now, in the Lord, you are all daylight. You must live as men native to the light." (Eph. 5.8.) There is a clear reference to baptism as an illumination in Hebrews (Heb. 6.4), and *phōtismos* (Greek for "illumination") was a name given to baptism in the early Church.

Next after creation comes the Deluge as a type of baptism.

The narrative of the Deluge in Genesis skilfully interweaves two distinct accounts that must have existed previously in separation. The first, the Yahwist account, sees the Deluge primarily as a destruction, a judgement on man's sinfulness; the second, the Priestly account, presents it as an act of divine saving power, leading to the covenant with Noah, the man God rescued from the wicked. Once more, then, water has two meanings: destruction and death on the one hand, and renewal and life on the other. This combination of meanings found in the waters of the Deluge is expressed perfectly in the prayer for the blessing of the font: "O God who by water didst wash away the crimes of a guilty world, and by the outpouring of the Flood didst signify regeneration, so that one and the same element might have the mysterious power to make an end of vice and a beginning of virtue; look down, O Lord, upon the face of thy Church and multiply within her thy acts of regeneration."

There is a passage in the Second-Isaias that sees the promised return from exile as repeating the saving intervention by which God rescued Noah. "If I abandoned thee, it was but for a little moment, and now, in my great compassion, I bring thee home again. Hid I my face from thee, it was for a short while, till my anger should be spent; love that takes pity on thee shall be eternal, says the Lord, thy ransomer. The days of Noe have come again; I swore to Noe that I would bring no more floods on the earth such as his; thou, too, hast my oath for it, I will be angry with thee no more, rebuke thee no more." (Isa.

54.7–9.) "The days of Noe have come again"—
this idea, which saw a new Deluge in the restoration of Israel, eventually led to the theology of baptism we find in the First Epistle of Peter. "God waited patiently in the days of Noah and the building of the ark, and in the ark a few persons, eight in all, were brought to safety through the water. This water prefigured the water of baptism through which you are now brought to safety. Baptism is not the washing away of bodily pollution, but the appeal made to God by a good conscience; and it brings salvation through the resurrection of Jesus Christ." (1 Pet. 3.20–21—New English Bible.) The waters of baptism swallow up a sinful world but give rise to a new world for those whom God brings to safety through them. This baptismal interpretation of the Deluge is most frequent in the Fathers, who elaborate further some of the details. The Ark is a figure of the Church, the dove of the Spirit. The number eight is given a symbolic interpretation, and Noah is taken as representing Christ. The narrative of the Deluge was formerly one of the readings on Easter Night.

If the Deluge is perhaps the most obvious of the baptismal types, the most important is certainly the Exodus. For the Israelites the deliverance from Egypt was the saving act of God *par excellence*. It remained in their minds as the type of all redemptive activity; what God had done for them in Egypt, at the Red Sea and in the desert was what they meant by redemption. When they looked forward to a new saving intervention by God they could not but conceive it as a new Exodus. And in looking back upon the first Exodus they rightly saw in the escape from Egypt the origin of their nation as a nation and in the covenant of Sinai the basis of their relation with God. Their appreciation of the Exodus was true. We are not dealing here with folklore, as we are with the Deluge. In the assessment of faith the raising up of Moses and his leading of the Israelites out of Egypt to be moulded into a nation in the desert and there bound by covenant to Yahweh its God was indeed the most important group of events before Christ. Here was an outstanding intervention of God in history, giving salvation in an initial form to the Israelites and preparing for the final salvation intended for all men. No wonder, then, that Christian tradition from the New Testament onwards has seen in the Exodus the pattern of God's saving activity, and therefore the type of Christ's work. Christ's death and resurrection are seen as a new Exodus in which Christ, leading us, passes from Egypt, that is, this world of sin and death ruled by the powers of darkness, to the promised land of the Resurrection and a new covenant with

God. Since baptism joins us to Christ in this
redemptive process, the Exodus becomes a type
of baptism, the waters of the Red Sea a figure of
the waters of baptism.

St. Paul gives this typology quite clearly when
he is reminding the Corinthians of the duties of
their Christian state: "Let me remind you,
brethren, of this. Our fathers were hidden, all of
them, under the cloud, and found a path, all of
them, through the sea; all alike, in the cloud and
in the sea, were baptized into Moses' fellowship.
They all ate the same prophetic food, and all
drank the same prophetic drink, watered by the
same prophetic rock which bore them company,
the rock that was Christ. And for all that, God
was ill pleased with most of them; see how they
were laid low in the wilderness. It is we that were
foreshadowed in these events." (1 Cor. 10.1–6.)
Thus, for St. Paul the passage through the Red
Sea is a figure of our baptism into Christ's fellowship, Moses being taken as a type of Christ. The
cloud is understood as the Spirit. Paul here follows a different tradition from that given in
Exodus and describes the cloud as covering the
people instead of going before them as a pillar;
it is the version we find in Psalm 104—"He
spread out a cloud to cover them". The manna
and the water from the rock are given a eucha-
ristic meaning.

With unmistakable clarity, then, the text from Paul gives us the central elements in the Exodus typology. Many other texts of the New Testament contain allusions to the same understanding of Christian initiation as a new Exodus, and this theme received a rich and detailed development in the catechetical writings of the Fathers.

It is the liturgy of Easter Night that gives this datum of tradition its living expression in the Church of today. During the Vigil we recall the Exodus as a figure of our redemption and celebrate our deliverance by Christ as the reality it prefigured. To quote the *Exsultet*: "This is the night on which thou didst first cause our forefathers, the sons of Israel, in their passage out of Egypt, to pass dry-shod over the Red Sea. This is the night which purged away the blackness of sin by the light of the fiery pillar. . . . On this night Christ burst the bonds of death and rose victorious from the grave. . . . Blessed indeed is the night, which despoiled the Egyptians and enriched the Hebrews! The night on which heaven is wedded to earth, the things of God to those of man!" The second of the four readings is the account of the Exodus, and the initial procession with the paschal candle is intended to evoke the march of the Israelites from Egypt under the guidance of the pillar of fire. The fact that this procession is also a mime of the Resurrection, symbolizing Christ's coming out of the darkness of the tomb into the splendour of his risen glory, reinforces the meaning of the Exodus as foreshadowing the death and resurrection of Christ.

Two sacraments enter into the structure of the Easter Vigil in the Roman rite: baptism and the Eucharist. By baptism the death-and-resurrection of Christ is realized in each of us, and so its celebration was brought into close association with Easter, the feast of that death and resurrection. When there are baptisms at the Vigil we celebrate the taking place of the paschal mystery in the new members of the Church and thus renew the grace of our own baptism before going with them to the altar to celebrate the Eucharist, which completes our union with Christ and with one another in Christ.

The death and resurrection of Christ is the new Pasch. Baptism is our initiation into this Pasch of Christ. So, baptism finds its prophetic type in the first Pasch. The Church sees the catechumen as in a similar position to the Israelites in Egypt, waiting to be led out of darkness and slavery across the waters of baptism to light and freedom, to the enjoyment of the manna of the Eucharist, membership of the People of God, a part in the Covenant and eventual entry into the Promised Land.

The Fathers saw a further type of baptism in the crossing of the Jordan under Joshua, because by baptism we are in a sense already within the Promised Land and in possession of the Kingdom. There is a possible allusion to this in the Gospel of John. The Evangelist makes a point of putting Christ beyond the Jordan before the miracle of the raising of Lazarus and notes that he went to "the place where John was when he first baptized". (John 10.40–1.) Christ therefore crossed the Jordan to go to Bethany and raise Lazarus from the dead, a miracle that has traditionally been given a baptismal meaning. The reference here to the first crossing of the Jordan and to baptism is admittedly obscure, but there are so many subtleties in John's Gospel that one hesitates to deny it. It is defended by good scholars, and it would explain the frequent use of the crossing of the Jordan and the resurrection of Lazarus in tradition in connection with baptism. The account of the raising of Lazarus was the Gospel text for one of the masses of the scrutinies.

I want to turn now from the types of baptism in the Old Testament to the actions, recorded in the New Testament, by which Christ established Christian baptism. The transition is not so sharp as it has often been made to appear. As we have seen, the Old-Testament types are not just illustrations; they constituted a real preparation for baptism, so that we can truly say that the process of making baptism began in the Old Testament. Again, some of the actions of Christ's public life looked forward as symbols to the sacraments of the Church in a way similar to that of the Old-Testament types. Nevertheless, Christ did more than foreshadow the sacraments; he took those decisive steps that founded them as realities of the Church's life. To use a familiar phrase, he instituted them.

The institution of the sacraments by Christ is frequently conceived inadequately. It is supposed that one can point to a single moment when Christ instituted each sacrament—before it the sacrament did not exist, after it the sacrament existed as a permanent institution. But this is to take the institution of a sacrament in an exclusively juridical fashion, as if it were the same kind of action as the signing of a legal contract. In fact several actions of Christ were usually involved in the process by which he established each sacrament and made known his will about it to the Apostles. Further, the establishment of the sacraments was but the element in the process by which Christ founded the Church, and it cannot be isolated from that. Finally, the death-and-resurrection is essential to the institution of every sacrament. Without it

2

the other acts of institution would have remained nugatory.

Christ began his making of baptism with his own baptism by John the Baptist in the Jordan. Tradition has always seen this as a decisive moment in the foundation of Christian baptism. In receiving the baptism of John publicly, Christ gave his approval to this baptism of repentance. But we must see a deeper significance in his action. John's baptism was an immediate preparation for Christian baptism. Christ received it to manifest what was to come and to inaugurate the work of bringing the new reality.

The baptism of Christ is recorded in all three Synoptics; it comes after their summaries of the Baptist's preaching: Matt. 3.13–17; Mark 1.9–11; Luke 3.21–2. The Fourth Gospel does not mention the baptism itself, but it describes the theophany that took place at it. We may take it, then, that the baptism of Christ is very firmly established as an historical fact. What believer would have later invented the story that the Lord Jesus had submitted to the baptism of John? Yet, in narrating the event, the Evangelists had also in mind Christian baptism. They bring out the significance of what occurred.

At Christ's baptism there was a manifestation of the Spirit. The Spirit of God descended like a dove. Why a dove? It recalls, as the Fathers pointed out, the Spirit hovering like a bird over the primeval waters, and the dove of the Deluge, which was a symbol of the Spirit. The Spirit is associated with a dove in rabbinical writings. A distinction was made in tradition between the Spirit as sanctifying the waters, which was referred to the sacrament of baptism, and the Spirit as anointing Christ, which was referred to the sacrament of confirmation.

Next, there was a designation of the Son by the Father. This is a reference to the messianic mission of Christ, but it announces also the adopted sonship of all the baptized.

The Spirit, Christ announced as Son, the Father: the scene at the Jordan was the presence and manifestation of the Trinity. The theophany took place at a baptism in water. Thus, all the elements that go to make up Christian baptism were displayed.

It is no wonder, then, that the Fathers insisted on the deep meaning of Christ's baptism in the Jordan and on its relevance to our baptism. It was there that the symbol of water, basically a natural human symbol but developed further under the Old Law, was brought within the Christian context. It was put into relation with the person and work of Christ. We may say that the water was consecrated then, not in the sense of receiving a permanent inherent power, but in the sense of being deputed to a sacred function, marked out for a new and sacred role, assumed into the mystery of Christ and the order of Christian salvation.

Although Christian baptism was thus revealed at the baptism of Christ, it derives its efficacy from his death and resurrection. But if we now examine the baptism of Christ more closely, we shall see that it indicates this. It looks forward to Christ's death and resurrection and in this way shows the connection between baptism and the paschal mystery.

The baptism of Jesus was the inauguration of his public ministry. It was a solemn messianic anointing. Not indeed that he was not Messiah and Son of God before, but this was a public declaration of his person and mission, standing at the beginning of his public life and marking the opening of his work.

Now, in the synoptic account, the voice from heaven proclaims: "Thou art my beloved Son; in thee I am well pleased." (Mark. 1.11.) This is a reference to the opening of the first of the Servant Songs (Isa. 42.1), the four songs in the Book of Isaias which deal with the Servant of Yahweh who must suffer for his people. The sentence therefore designates Jesus as the Servant who takes the sins of his people upon himself in his suffering and death. Jesus, who is innocent himself, undergoes the baptism of repentance because he has come to bear our sins and will die for our redemption.

The baptism in the River Jordan was a sign pointing to his death. The waters of the Jordan represented the waters of chaos and destruction, the waters of death and dissolution. But Christ went into them in strength, not in weakness. He went into them of his own will. He overcame them: they did not overcome him. As we shall see in a moment, the humiliation of the descent into them was followed by the glorification of the ascent from them.

That the baptism of Christ was a symbol of his redemptive death is confirmed by the sayings in which Christ speaks of his death as a baptism. "There is a baptism I must needs be baptized with, and how impatient am I for its accomplishment!" (Luke 12.50.) Again, Jesus said to the sons of Zebedee: "You do not know what it is you ask. Have you strength to drink of the cup I am to drink of, to be baptized with the baptism I am to be baptized with?" (Mark 10.38.) The baptism in the Jordan prefigured the baptism of Calvary; it was the beginning of the messianic work that reached its culmination in the death on the Cross.

The Fourth Gospel makes the connection between the baptism of Jesus and his death even clearer. The baptism itself is not mentioned but the theophany is, and John the Baptist declares that it was through this that he knew who Christ was. This connects what he says about Christ with the happenings at the baptism. And this is how he designates Christ: "Look, this is the Lamb of God; look, this is he who takes away the sins of the world." (John 1.29.) John here bears witness that Jesus is both the new paschal lamb, antitype of the lamb that was the perennial symbol of Israel's deliverance from Egypt, and the Suffering Servant of Yahweh, who was compared to a lamb in his patient endurance of death for the sins of many. (Isa. 53.7.) So, in the baptism was revealed the death of Christ.

But at the Jordan the humiliation of the baptism of repentance was followed by a glorification. "So Jesus was baptized, and as he came straight up out of the water, suddenly heaven was opened, and he saw the Spirit of God coming down like a dove and resting upon him. And with that, a voice came from heaven, which said, This is my beloved Son, in whom I am well pleased." (Matt. 3.16–7.) Jesus came up out of the Jordan as he was later to rise from the tomb. He came up from the waters of death in the glory of the Spirit. His divine sonship was manifested here as it was manifested in power by his resurrection. The heavens were opened at the

Jordan; they would be opened for all men when he ascended to sit at the right hand of his Father. The baptism of Christ was the promise of what was to come. The waters of the Jordan represent the waters of a new creation, made to serve by the triumphant strength of Christ.

The baptism of Christ, which opened his public ministry, was therefore related to the essential moment of the death and resurrection. It formed as it were a preliminary sketch. That this anticipation of the drama of redemption took place in a ritual with water is significant. Christ rehearsed for his death and resurrection by entering the waters of baptism and emerging from them. Men take part in his death and resurrection by doing the same.

But before men could be taken up by baptism into Christ's death and resurrection, that sacred mystery had to be accomplished in fact. That baptism as a sacrament depends upon the death and resurrection of Christ for its existence is a truth that flows from the theology of redemption, and it must be taken for granted here. Mention must be made, however, of how John in his Gospel indicates the relation of the sacraments to Christ's death on Calvary. I refer to his account of the piercing of Christ's side after his death: "One of the soldiers opened his side with a spear; and immediately blood and water flowed out. He who saw it has borne his witness; and his witness is worthy of trust. He tells what he knows to be the truth, that you, like him, may learn to believe." (John 19.34–5.) John attaches great importance to this incident, as is shown by his insistence on his own veracity as an eye-witness. Plainly, then, the water and blood flowing from Christ's side have a deep meaning for him. Many Fathers saw in them symbols of the two sacraments of baptism and the Eucharist. This is probably not the only level of meaning in John. The blood may well be a sign of the reality of Christ's humanity and of his sacrifice, the water a symbol of the Spirit and of the sacrifice's spiritual fruitfulness. But in view of the sacramental bearing of so much in John's Gospel, the meaning of the water as baptism and of the blood as the Eucharist may be reasonably taken as also intended.

To grasp the full teaching of the text, it must be remembered that throughout his Gospel John presents Christ's death as the first step in his glorification. He sees the death and resurrection as one. Christ was lifted up in glory on the Cross. Now, when he describes the actual death of Christ, he uses a peculiar expression. Instead of the usual idiomatic phrases found in the Synoptics, he writes, "he handed over [*paredōken*] the Spirit". He saw in Christ's last breath the first giving of the Spirit—the Spirit that was not given until Christ had been glorified, according to John's own testimony. (John 7.39.) Thus, in recording the scene on Calvary, he associates together the Spirit given by Christ now gone to his glory, baptism and the Eucharist. It is in fact by these two sacraments that the Spirit coming from the risen Christ is communicated to men.

After his resurrection, Christ, now exalted and possessed of his complete power, sent out the Apostles to baptize all men and make them his disciples: "All authority in heaven and on earth, he said, has been given to me; you, therefore, must go out, making disciples of all nations, and baptizing them in the name of the Father, and of the Son, and of the Holy Ghost, teaching them to observe all the commandments which I have given you." (Matt. 28.18–20; see also Mark 16. 15–16.) The Apostles, however, did not begin to baptize until after Pentecost. It was necessary for them first to wait for the full outpouring of the Spirit which came on that day. They themselves had first to receive the "baptism with the Holy Spirit", as the experience of Pentecost is called in Acts (1.5), before communicating the Spirit to others by the sacramental rite. The descent of the Spirit at Pentecost finished the creation of the Church and, consequently, completed the making of baptism. The Apostles, now fully aware of their mission and their powers, began to preach and to baptize.

Thus, the history of the making of baptism, which goes back in a sense to creation itself, came to an end on Pentecost Day, and on that day began the long history of its celebration by the Church. But the past history of its making is not now irrelevant, because it shows us the meaning of the sacrament and because each baptism is really created anew and gives us a part in the events that first made it.

THE CHURCH AND HER RITES

To the crowd that gathered near the house on Pentecost Day Peter preached his first sermon, proclaiming to the people the message of our salvation in Christ. "When they heard this," we read in the Acts, "their consciences were stung; and they asked Peter and his fellow apostles, Brethren, what must we do? Repent, Peter said to them, and be baptized, every one of you, in the name of Jesus Christ, to have your sins forgiven; then you will receive the gift of the Holy Spirit." And that is what they did in large numbers. St. Luke tells us, "So all those who had taken his words to heart were baptized, and about three thousand souls were won for the Lord that day." (Acts 2.37–41.) The celebration of the new rite of Christian baptism had begun.

The position of the original group of disciples was unique. I am referring to the Apostles and others who formed a company of about a hundred and twenty and who underwent together the experience of Pentecost. They were not themselves baptized except with the baptism of John. Luke makes this clear when he records these words spoken by Christ before the Ascension: "John's baptism, I told you, was with water, but there is a baptism with the Holy Spirit which you are to receive, not many days from this." (Acts 1.5.) The first Christians were baptized in the fires of Pentecost. By the personal work of Christ they had been made into a community and constituted as the Church of the New Testament. This work was completed by the sending of the Spirit at Pentecost. So, these first disciples were made Christians and initiated as members of the Church, with all the powers and graces that this implies, in a special way. The events they had experienced made them the new People of God, the messianic community, the Church of Christ. They recognized this at Pentecost, but their actions after Pentecost show that they were also aware that they could join others to their fellowship by baptism and the laying on of hands or confirmation. These two sacramental rites made others members of the new Church and imparted to them the salvation brought by Christ and his gift of the Spirit. Baptism began as the rite by which others were admitted to membership of the original apostolic community.

The practice of the first Christians of baptizing those who joined their fellowship is an indubitable fact. There is mention of baptisms in all the various literary sources that modern criticism distinguishes in the Acts of the Apostles. The great epistles of Paul, which were written only about twenty years after the death of Christ, present baptism as firmly established, not as something recently introduced. Besides, Paul himself was baptized on his conversion (Acts 9.18), so baptism was not of his making. There is, then, no reasonable doubt but that the sacrament of baptism comes from the personal initiative of Christ. We have already seen how this fact is presented in the Gospels.

The New Testament does not give us any detailed information about the manner of baptism. The word "baptize", which means "dip" or "immerse", and the connection with John's baptism, suggest immersion in some form or other. St. Paul calls baptism a bath of water (Eph. 5.26) and a bath of regeneration (Titus 3.5), and the great passage in Romans that describes baptism as a burial with Christ (Rom. 6.4) is usually taken as implying a rite of submersion or total immersion, although, as I shall point out, this is not so clear as is commonly supposed. A text in the Acts gives us a more definite indication of the manner of baptism. It is the account of the baptism of the Ethiopian by Philip the Deacon. "Both of them," we read, "Philip and the eunuch, went down into the water, and Philip

baptized him there. But when they came up from
the water, Philip was carried off by the spirit of
the Lord." This was certainly some form of immersion. There is no clear evidence in the New
Testament for the practice of affusion or pouring, but it can be argued that the situation in
which Paul baptized the jailer and his household
at Philippi (Acts 16.33) makes it unlikely that
the rite of immersion was followed. The *Did-
ache*, of uncertain date though usually taken as a
work of the early second century, expressly
allows a mere pouring where there is a lack of
water, and other evidence supports this.

It is, then, generally agreed that in the early
Church the normal practice, which lasted up to
the fourteenth century, was immersion, but that
affusion was freely used where necessary, notably
in the baptism of the sick. (The third form of
ablution, namely sprinkling, which is admitted
as valid though discouraged in canon law, has no
ancient warrant.) Now, it used to be assumed
that the immersion practised was always total;
but this assumption has had to be modified to
meet the archaeological evidence. Representa-
tions of baptism in the frescoes of the Catacombs
and on sarcophagi do not indicate a rite of submersion. The person is shown standing in shallow water while water is being poured over his
head. There is no hint of any plunging below

the surface; the rite seems to have been a combination of partial immersion and affusion. This conclusion is supported by the size of the fonts that have survived. These are usually pools sunk below the level of the floor, and the candidates went down into them by steps; but they are only two to four feet in depth and too small in diameter to allow submersion by lying down. A further fact that must be taken into account is that baptisteries were sometimes provided with a spout of water similar to that found in the public baths. The minister, it seems, baptized the candidate by guiding his head under the jet or by directing the flow over the head by means of a shallow vessel; and so, where there was no jet he would have used such a vessel to throw water from the pool over the head. Once again the conclusion is that the rite was a combination of partial immersion and affusion. How does this fit in with the Pauline comparison of baptism to a burial? Does not the comparison prove that total immersion was at least the primitive practice? In reference to this it has been pointed out that in the ancient burial rites the main feature was the throwing of a few handfuls of earth upon the corpse. Since that was so, the throwing of water over the candidate made a satisfactory symbol of burial. In ancient practice, then, there was no clear distinction between immersion and affusion, and the rite seems to have generally been a combination of the two. When, however, from the sixth century onwards, baptisms for the most part were infant baptisms, total immersion became the norm; it is still the rite followed in the East. It was replaced in the West by affusion about the fourteenth century, although the practice of immersion is found sporadically for some time after this. It is never in fact used now in the Roman rite, but it is still allowed for in the liturgical books.

As was to be expected, in the first period of the Church's history baptisms were carried out in rivers or lakes, or even in the sea; flowing water was preferred. Soon baths in large private houses were also used. Even before the peace of the Church under Constantine, special places were reserved for baptism, but it was only after that time, the first part of the fourth century, that baptisteries began to be multiplied. Where found, the baptistery is set apart from the main hall used for the celebration of the Eucharist. In Greece and North Africa it is an adjoining room; in Syria and Italy a detached building. In both cases, the baptisteries take their shape from the contemporary mausolea, the fonts imitate sarcophagi, and the decorations are similar to those used on these monuments. This custom reflects the belief that baptism is a burial with Christ.

The reason for detached baptisteries was the separation insisted upon between catechumens and the faithful. The assembly hall of the faithful was not the place for the rite casting out the darkness of paganism. When adult baptisms became rare and the catechumenate disappeared, the font was placed within the church—near the door, because baptism is the gateway to the Church and the other sacraments.

At the beginning of the third century Tertullian mentions that the water for baptism is blessed, and in the middle of that century St. Cyprian insists upon this. Both represent the Church in North Africa. Tertullian, in his remarks, takes the practice for granted, so that it must have already existed for some time. We can conclude, then, that from the second half of the second century the Church in North Africa knew a special rite calling down the blessing of God on the water before it was used in baptism. There are indications that such a rite existed elsewhere in the Church at the same time. Rome, however, seems to have adopted the practice later than other Churches, because, at least according to the more probable reconstruction of the text, there is no mention of it in the *Apostolic Tradition* of Hippolytus, which reflects Roman practice at the beginning of the third century. After the first references and allusions nothing more is said about this blessing until the fourth century. But then and afterwards abundant testimonies are available from both East and West, which show the importance attached to this rite. We do not know exactly when Rome took up the practice, but it is highly likely it had it in the fourth century, when St. Ambrose was writing about it, with great emphasis, in Milan. In any case the present prayer for the consecration of the water is quoted in part in the fifth century by St. Peter Chrysologus.

The Fathers regard the blessing of the water as part of the baptismal rite and speak of it as if it were necessary for the sacrament. Baptism consists of the blessing of the water, and then the application of the sanctified element to the candidate, together with the invocation of the Trinity. Yet, baptism in ordinary water, used as this was in cases of necessity, was always considered valid. It is not difficult to reconcile these two points of teaching. The essential sacramental action, including the words that are part of it, itself sanctifies the element it uses. The water is marked out as a thing of God, purified and made holy, by being used in a sacramental gesture and associated with the sacred words of the sacrament. In other words, the sanctification of the water chosen for use is part of the meaning of the sacrament and is implicitly expressed by the essential minimum of the rite. But it is the custom of the Church to display the meaning of the sacrament more fully by further prayers and secondary rites. The rite of blessing the water expresses the truth more fully that in the sacrament God makes holy a material element for his sacred purpose. In the prayers of blessing we find a twofold meaning: there is an exorcism to remove the water from the domain of the devil; this is followed by a positive consecration to give the water power to bring forth new life.

In the East the water is consecrated for each baptism, and for cases of necessity a short blessing is provided. This makes it very clear that the rite of blessing the water is an integral part of the sacramental sign. The Easterns never used the baptismal water outside the sacrament; hence they did not keep it after use. The custom arose in the West of using the consecrated baptismal water in various ways apart from the sacrament, as we still do at Easter, calling the baptismal water Easter water. This led to the keeping of the water and the separation of the blessing of the water from the baptism itself when baptisms were no longer confined to Easter Night. The disadvantage of this is that people forget that the rite of consecrating the water is part of the baptismal rite, which we must know if we are to appreciate the Church's understanding of the sacrament. No Catholic should be unfamiliar with it.

The blessing of the baptismal water is an important feature of the Easter Vigil in the Roman rite. The long consecratory prayer in its present form is already found in the sixth century in the *Gelasian Sacramentary,* except for the fact that Alcuin in the eighth century added the dialogue and introduction that turned the prayer into a preface. I have already said that part of the prayer was quoted in the previous century. The text as it stands is a compilation of texts of different origins. The various ceremonies carried out during it have been introduced at different times. In the seventh century in Rome the only action was the plunging into the water of the two candles that accompanied the celebrant; it was done to symbolize the descent of the Holy Spirit like light. Later the paschal candle was used instead of the two candles and the ceremony changed its meaning somewhat: the thought was principally of Christ. Another early rite is the dividing of the water in the form of a cross, a consecratory gesture of signing. The other actions were added when the Roman rite came to Gaul. It was there also that there was added after the prayer the rite of consecrating the water by pouring in the sacred oils. This was originally a way of perfuming the water; it became a symbol of the descent of the Spirit and a link joining baptism to the bishop, who consecrates the oils. More important than the various actions is the wording of the prayer, which is rich in texture, bringing together many of the traditional themes concerning baptism.

In the early Church, when the candidates came to the place of baptism they stripped off their clothes and were baptized stark naked. The custom had its origin in the practical requirements for baptism as then administered by immersion or by immersion with affusion. It also fitted into the cultural context. In the Mediterranean countries people were used to the custom of nakedness in the public baths, and propriety was not so easily offended as it would now be. Provision was made for decency by some segregation of men and women. The women, too, were assisted by deaconesses, who helped with the anointing, though they did not administer the baptism. Practical though it was in origin, the Fathers gave the stripping-off of clothes and the return to nakedness a symbolic meaning. It signified the putting-off of the old man and his works; clothes were symbols of the passions and of mortality. It was an imitation of Christ, who hung naked on the Cross and by his nakedness overcame principalities and powers; the candidate by his nakedness shakes off the hold the evil powers have on him. Finally, it was a return to the primitive innocence of our first parents. Despite the teaching thus attached to it, the northern peoples never took to the custom. It is, in fact, a good example of how the Church works within a given outlook.

So far we have been dealing with the first constituent of the central rite of baptism: water and its use. Now we must consider the second constituent, which is essential to complete the first: the words or form. The history of the baptismal form is still disputed among scholars. The view I shall follow here is the more common, and I also find it more convincing. Its distinctive tenet is that in the early centuries there was no form in the sense in which we now have it, as a formula pronounced over the candidate by the minister. What happened at baptism was a profession of faith by the candidate in answer to an interrogation by the minister.

Faith and baptism are closely linked in the New Testament. St. Paul writes: "Through faith in Christ Jesus you are all now God's sons. All you who have been baptized in Christ's name have put on the person of Christ." (Gal. 3.26-7.) This connection between faith and baptism is made particularly clear in the Acts of the Apostles. Thus, "Philip came and preached to them about God's kingdom. Then they found faith and were baptized, men and women alike, in the name of Jesus Christ." (Acts 8.12.) Again, "Crispus, the ruler of the synagogue, learned to believe in the Lord, and so did all his household; and by now many of the Corinthians listened and found faith, and were baptized." (Acts 18.8.) Baptism is associated with professing the Faith.

In the references to baptism in the Acts mention is made a number of times of being baptized in the name of Jesus Christ or of the Lord Jesus. The question of baptism in the name of Jesus has long been discussed among theologians. What does the phrase mean? It does not indicate the existence in the apostolic Church of a baptismal form, "I baptize thee in the name of Jesus", corresponding to our present trinitarian formula. Development subsequent to the New Testament suggests that there was no such baptismal form, whether mentioning Christ or the Trinity. No, what the phrase means is that when he was baptized the person professed his faith in Jesus. This is the bearing of the words with which Ananias told Saul to be baptized—"Rise up and be baptized and wash away thy sins, invoking his name."(Acts 22.16.) The person invoked the name of Christ by some declaration of faith in him and willingness to follow him.

How was this faith expressed? In the apostolic Church the name of Christ did not mean the name Jesus, but the name Lord, *Kyrios,* given to Christ in his exaltation. This is what St. Paul is referring to when he writes in the Epistle to the Philippians: "That is why God has raised him to such a height, given him that name which is greater than any other name; so that everything in heaven and on earth and under the earth must bend the knee before the name of Jesus, and every tongue must confess Jesus Christ as the Lord, dwelling in the glory of God the Father." (Phil. 2.9–11.) The name given to Christ at his resurrection was the divine name, Yahweh or, in its Greek equivalent, *Kyrios.* The acclamation, "Jesus is the Lord", was a popular credal formula, which expressed faith in the divinity of Christ and in his role as the glorified Saviour, the source of the Spirit. Such was the content of the baptismal faith and the significance of baptism in the name of Jesus, even if the formula varied. The only text that gives us the wording of a baptismal profession of faith is an interpolation. It comes, however, from a very ancient baptismal interrogation and probably belongs to the apostolic age. It is Verse 37 of Chapter 8 of Acts: "Philip said, If thou dost believe with all thy heart, thou mayest [be baptized]. And he answered, I believe that Jesus Christ is the Son of God."

To profess one's faith in Jesus as Lord is to profess one's faith in the Father and the Spirit. It was the Father who bestowed the divine name *Kyrios* on the Son, and the Spirit is the gift of the glorified Jesus. As Peter put it in his sermon on Pentecost Day: "God, then, has raised up this man, Jesus, from the dead; we are all witnesses of it. And now, exalted at God's right hand, he has claimed from his Father his promise to bestow the Holy Spirit; and he has poured out that Spirit, as you can see and hear for yourselves." (Acts 2.32–3.) The Christian faith has always been trinitarian, though there was less need with the first Jewish converts than with the later Gentile converts to state expressly the role of the Father. At the end of Matthew's Gospel, in the command to baptize we find a trinitarian formula: "You, therefore, must go out, making disciples of all nations, and baptizing them in the name of the Father, and of the Son, and of the Holy Ghost." (Matt. 28.19.) This reflects liturgical usage and shows that some time before the Greek Matthew was written in the last decades of the first century what was implicit about the Trinity in the earlier baptismal professions of faith had been made explicit. The text is not quoting a baptismal form, but stating the object of the baptized person's profession of faith.

In the centuries immediately following the New Testament, when baptisms were still chiefly adult baptisms, the essential rite continued to comprise a profession of faith and an immersion. It is impossible to set out the arguments for that here. But this is how the rite is described in the *Apostolic Tradition* of Hippolytus, and in the works of St. Ambrose. The first shows us the Roman rite at the beginning of the third century, though admittedly the difficulties of reconstructing the text make its witness on this point open to question. St. Ambrose's testimony directly concerns fourth-century Milan, but the relation between Milan and Rome makes it relevant to the Roman rite.[1] Both give the same picture of baptism. The candidate and minister both go down into the water. The minister lays his hand upon the candidate and asks him in turn about his faith in the Father, the Son and the Holy Spirit. Each time the candidate answers, "I believe" to the question, and immediately with his hand on the head the minister dips him in the water. There is thus an interrogatory creed—similar to the kind still found in our

[1] The relevant passages are given in a handy collection of documents by E. C. Whitaker, *Documents of the Baptismal Liturgy*, London, S.P.C.K. (1960).

baptismal rite immediately before the actual baptism but here at the very centre of the rite instead of a form—a triple profession of faith and a triple immersion.

The change in the structure of the central baptismal action came about when infant baptism became the rule and adult baptism infrequent. The recipient was made passive in the baptism itself. The questions of the minister and the answers of the candidate were replaced by a formula pronounced by the minister alone. The change took place at various times in different Churches from the fourth to the seventh centuries. It occurred later in Rome than elsewhere; the change had not been made in the sixth century but it is certainly found in the eighth. The form used henceforward in the Roman rite is too familiar to repeat. The baptismal form used by the Greeks runs: "The servant of God N . . . is baptized, in the name of the Father, and of the Son, and of the Holy Spirit. Amen."

It should perhaps be remarked before leaving the question of the form that what was once valid is not necessarily so now. The Church has power to change, not the meaning of a sacramental symbol, but the manner in which that meaning is to be expressed. It is therefore for

the Church to say which rites she recognizes as
her sacraments here and now.

Hippolytus tells us that after the baptism the
neophytes were anointed with chrism. He is the
first to speak of this post-baptismal anointing
distinct from confirmation. I shall come back to
it later because it is more convenient to discuss
it together with confirmation.

When they had been baptized and anointed,
the neophytes put on a white garment before
going to the bishop to be confirmed and afterwards taking part in the Eucharist. The white
garment was worn at liturgical assemblies during
Easter week until the Saturday, when it was laid
aside. The prayer which is now said when the
garment—or the miserable piece of cloth that
usually takes its place—is handed over goes back
to the eighth century and is of Gallican origin.
It does not tell us much about the meaning of
the garment; for this we must go to the writings
of the Fathers. These saw several related meanings in it. The white garment replaced the
clothes left aside before baptism. Since these
had symbolized the old man, the white garment
was a symbol of the new man. In other words, it
is a sign of baptismal grace, which was explained
as involving purity of soul and bodily incorrupti-
bility. This grace is a share in the glory of Christ.
This glory was shown at the Transfiguration,

and we are told that then Christ's garments
became as white as snow. (Matt. 17.2.) The baptismal robe recalls the garments of the trans-
figured Christ and in that way reminds us that
by baptism we share the glory of the risen Christ,
since the Transfiguration was an anticipation of
the Resurrection. Baptism is, as St. Paul tells us,
a putting on of Christ. (Gal. 3.27.) Another interpretation sees the white garment as the restoration of primitive integrity. It was developed in
this way. Before the Fall, man, though naked in
body, was clothed with grace and innocence as
in a garment of light. Sin stripped man and left
him exposed. Baptism covered his nakedness
once more. Some also find an allusion in the
white garment to the priestly status of Christians. The priests of the Old Testament wore
vestments of white linen, and in the Apocalypse
the twenty-four elders around the throne, who
are shown as celebrating a heavenly liturgy, are
clothed in white garments. The baptized share
the priesthood of Christ, and they put on white
garments before joining in the Eucharist, which
brings to earth the liturgy of heaven. Finally,
the white garment prefigures our future glory.

We can order the various elements of the symbolism of the white garments into a coherent
whole. They refer first to Adam and to his state
of innocence in Paradise before the Fall. They

point next to Christ, the Second Adam, who came to restore the grace lost by the first. Hence they signify our sharing in the grace of Christ. And lastly they symbolically anticipate the glory to come, especially our resurrection.

In our present rite the giving of the white garment is followed by the presentation of a lighted candle to the neophyte. In the early centuries there is mention of the lights carried by the newly baptized, but our present ceremony of giving the candle came in about the eleventh century. It is a beautiful closing of the baptismal rite. The lighted candle reminds us of Easter and the paschal candle. In some places in recent years the practice has grown up of keeping the paschal candle in the baptistery and lighting the candle from it at the baptism. This candle, like the paschal candle, is the image of the risen Christ and of our share in his resurrection; for Christ is the light of the world. The prayer used in giving it tells us that the flame of baptism must be kept burning within us, and that we must persevere like the wise virgins of the parable so that we may meet Christ in the marriage feast of heaven.

Up to the present we have been considering the central rite of baptism and the short sequel to this. But the actual baptism is preceded by a long series of preparatory rites, which were originally spread out over a period of preparation. To understand them it is helpful to know something of their history.

Adult baptism has always presupposed some preparation on the part of the person to be baptized. As the New Testament presents it, baptism follows preaching and demands a first faith in the message, repentance and acceptance of Christian morality. At the beginning, however, these requirements were not secured by any formal arrangements. About the middle of the second century St. Justin gives us a glimpse of what was done to prepare candidates for baptism. The preparation consists of two things: teaching, both doctrinal and moral, and the practice of prayer and fasting. No details are given about the way the preparation was organized. But when we come to the beginning of the third century, we have a full account of the preparation, which was definitely organized by then, in the *Apostolic Tradition* of Hippolytus.

The preparation for baptism was divided into two stages. There was the remote preparation, during which the candidates were known as catechumens, a word meaning "those under instruction", and which we therefore call the catechumenate; and then came the proximate preparation, when the catechumens became the *electi*, or those chosen out for baptism.

A person who wanted to become a catechumen had to be brought along to the representatives of the Church by a Christian who vouched for him. He was questioned about his way of life and his motive in becoming a Christian. If the examination proved satisfactory, he was accepted as a catechumen. The catechumenate normally lasted three years, but it could be shortened if the person's earnestness and conduct justified this. The period was not so much a time of instruction in doctrine—that came later—but of moral testing. It was a kind of novitiate in which the catechumen was tried and trained in the practice of the Christian moral life. Hippolytus tells us that the person was given over to a teacher but he does not give us any details about the content of the instructions. We know from elsewhere that these consisted mainly in readings from certain books of Scripture that contained suitable moral instruction, such as Esther, Judith, Tobias and the Wisdom writings. Each session ended with prayer and the teacher, who was sometimes a layman, gave a blessing by laying his hands upon the catechumens—this was the earlier form of blessing. Catechumens were allowed to take part also in the readings and sermons of the community assemblies.

When the three years were up, the catechumens were again examined about their moral conduct, and this had also to be attested by those who recommended them. Then began the proximate preparation, which took place (although Hippolytus himself does not tell us this) in the time before Easter, because already from the second century baptisms were done in common on Easter Night. The preparation consisted in a more systematic instruction, this time doctrinal in character. The catechumens heard the Gospel, or good news of salvation. Daily an exorcism was pronounced over them, with the imposition of hands. As the time of baptism drew near, the bishop gave a more solemn exorcism to make certain they were purified. On the Thursday they had to take a bath in readiness for the baptism. On the Friday and the Saturday they fasted. During the Saturday there was an assembly of all those who were to be baptized, presided over by the bishop. They all prayed and knelt, the bishop exorcized them again by a laying on of hands, breathed on their faces, signed their foreheads, ears and noses, and then bade them rise. That night came the Vigil. It lasted the whole night and included readings and instructions. At cock-crow they went to the place of baptism and undressed. Then came the renunciation of Satan and the anointing with the oil of exorcism, which we now call the oil of catechumens. Baptism followed.

3

In the fourth and fifth centuries the preparation for baptism was further developed. It was the age of mass conversions and called for some changes. The division, however, into two stages still remained. Our concern here is with the evolution of the Roman rite.

The entry into the catechumenate was made more elaborate. More instruction was given at the outset in the rudiments of the Faith, and especially in the commandments to be observed. Some ceremonies were added: an "exsufflation", which means a breathing to blow away Satan, the imposition of the sign of the cross, the blessing and giving of salt and a final formula of blessing that looked forward to baptism and the Eucharist, namely the prayer *Deus Patrum* ("God of our fathers"), which still closes the first part of our baptismal rite. The catechumenate still in theory lasted three years, but many were content to stay catechumens for most of their lives and they were allowed to call themselves Christians.

The second stage in the preparation still began with an examination of the moral conduct of the catechumen. If this was satisfactory, he was put on the list of *electi*; the inscribing of the name was accompanied by a prayer. This was at the beginning of Lent, and the proximate preparation took place in the setting of Lent, as it had by then developed. It was a time of moral and doctrinal instruction, together with a great spiritual effort on the part of the candidates by the more careful observance of the Commandments and much fasting. The whole Christian community, at the same time, was trying to live the Christian life more intensely in a similar way.

But the Church did not think of this preparation as being simply a matter of the personal efforts of the candidates. They needed the help of God, particularly to break the hold of Satan, who would compromise the work if he could. Hence the establishment of the rites known as scrutinies. The word "scrutiny" suggests an examination of the candidates, but the word did not in fact mean a testing of their knowledge so much as a testing and repressing of the power of Satan. The word can also bear the sense of penetrating, so that it would refer here to the penetrating or transforming action of God. The idea of the scrutinies was certainly that of giving the candidates the help they needed to support their personal struggles. The scrutinies, then, were exorcisms, consisting of kneelings, prayers, the signing of the candidates with the sign of the cross and the laying on of hands. Distinct formularies were used for men and women. There were three scrutinies at this time, held on the third, fourth and fifth Sundays of Lent respectively. Mass followed the scrutinies; the candidates attended the first part, and the Mass texts were specially chosen to go with the scrutinies.

At the third scrutiny, which was held on the fifth Sunday of Lent, later called Passion Sunday, took place the ceremony of the *Traditio Symboli*, the handing over of the Apostles' Creed. The Creed was recited in the presence of the candidates and a general explanation of it given to them by the celebrant. From now until Easter they received a series of detailed instructions on it and were expected to learn it by heart. On the morning of Holy Saturday the *electi* were gathered together in a special assembly. There was a final exorcism and they were anointed with the oil of catechumens on the ears, nose and breast. This anointing was accompanied by the *Ephpheta* formula, still in use. After the anointing came the renunciation of Satan and then the ceremony of the *Redditio Symboli*, the giving back of the Creed. The candidates were expected to recite the Creed in front of the bishop. They then dispersed and came back later for the Easter Vigil and baptism.

At the beginning of the sixth century there was a simplification in the preparation for baptism. The first stage or catechumenate disappeared. The reason was that the influence of the Church had by now changed the social environment, so that the long time of probation before admitting a convert was unnecessary. The ceremonies for the entry into the catchumenate and for the inscription of the name on the list of *electi* were not suppressed. They were all joined to the first scrutiny. The second scrutiny remained unchanged, but at this time the third scrutiny, when the Creed was handed over, had a similar ceremony added to it of handing over the Lord's Prayer.

Later in the sixth century a much more drastic change took place in the organization of baptism. This was due to the fact that baptisms now were mainly of infants. The Church had always baptized infants. Hippolytus tells us that infants were baptized before the grown-ups. That was on Easter Night. We know from St. Cyprian, Bishop of Carthage in the third century, that Christian parents were expected to have their babies baptized immediately, without waiting even for the eighth day after birth, as some were doing in imitation of the rite of circumcision. Infants, therefore, were baptized without any formal preparation, whether at Easter or at other times. But, despite the opposition of the bishops, the custom became widespread of delaying baptism. The idea was that the difficulties of youth should be overcome before undertaking the obligations of the Christian state, so that in this way baptismal innocence would not be endangered. The sacrament of penance was an arduous business in those days, and moreover was available only once for each person. By the sixth century infant baptism was again regularly administered and adult baptism had become comparatively rare. But now the days specified for adult baptism (chiefly Easter, but Pentecost and later the Epiphany had been added) were set apart also for infant baptism, which outside necessity was given only on those days. In Rome in the sixth century the preparatory rites of baptism were reorganized to adapt them to infants.

In this reorganization the scrutinies were increased to seven. It was thought to offset the passiveness of the recipients in this way and provide an increased divine intervention, and at the same time to show that here all was the work of grace. To get the number of seven scrutinies, recalling the seven gifts of the Holy Spirit, the final assembly of candidates on Holy Saturday morning was counted as a scrutiny. The first six scrutinies, corresponding to the original three, were no longer held on Sundays. Since only infants were involved, the intervention of the community was less important. They were at first transferred to the Wednesday, Friday and Saturday of the third and fourth weeks of Lent. It was then that the present masses for those days, with their references to baptism, were composed, and among the Scripture readings are to be found the passages, such as the account of the Samaritan woman and that of the man born blind, formerly used on the Sundays when the scrutinies were held. The *Traditio Symboli* took place on the second of the Wednesdays; by this time a ceremony of handing over the Gospels had been added to it, taking the place, as it were, of the instructions that were given to the adults. The handing over of the Lord's Prayer occurred on the second of the two Saturdays. On both those days, the Wednesday and Saturday of the fourth week in Lent, the masses have an extra lesson, taken from the Old Testament. Later on the first six scrutinies became more or less independent of the Lenten masses. The first and the third remained attached to the Wednesday and Saturday of the third week in Lent, with the third now counted as the second, but the other four were no longer fixed to a definite day; their date depended on the decision of the celebrant. The seventh was still held on the Holy Saturday morning.

Subsequent centuries saw a further simplification of this discipline. In the eighth century there were only three assemblies in preparation for baptism, the one on Holy Saturday morning and two previous meetings, one for the giving of the blessed salt and one for the rite of handing over the Gospel. All the rest had been dropped. The meetings were then reduced to two. In the tenth century, apart from the assembly on Holy Saturday, there was but one preliminary meeting, during which were performed the ancient rites of the first scrutiny, which came, it will be remembered, from the ceremony of making a catechumen.

Finally, in the eleventh and twelfth centuries was re-established the custom of baptizing infants immediately after their birth. This practice had become general by the thirteenth century. It led to the dropping of all the special meetings in preparation for baptism. The rites preceding baptism were not abolished. They were compressed into one ceremony carried out for each infant on the occasion of the baptism. This arrangement is already found in the eleventh century; it gradually became general, though as late as the twelfth and thirteenth centuries some of the Lenten scrutinies were held for infants in some of the larger churches. The main baptismal ritual in its compressed form also varied from place to place.

The *Rituale Romanum*, which is still in force, was first issued by Pope Paul V in 1614. In regard to baptism, it was based on a previous work, the *Liber Sacerdotalis*, a collection of rites

published by the Dominican Albert Castellani in
1523. A Bull issued by Leo X and dated 1520
had imposed this book on the Latin Church, but
the Pope died before the book was actually published and the Bull did not take effect. Castellani
drew up two alternative rituals for baptism,
both of which he intended for infant baptism.
The prayers and ceremonies were taken from
earlier sources, and most of the texts used go back
to the *Gelasian Sacramentary*, a book that takes
us back to the fifth and sixth centuries. The
texts were written originally for adults, and it is
a fact that, although the Church has adapted the
rite for infants, she has not yet composed special
texts for them. The *Roman Ritual* took over the
two formularies of Castellani, with but slight
modifications. But it assigned the first, shorter
ritual to the baptism of infants and made the
second, longer one the rite for the baptism of
adults. We do not use the rite for adult baptism
in this country. For use on a single occasion it is
long and involves much repetition. By a special
privilege we use the ritual for infants in baptizing an unbaptized convert.

It is generally agreed that the drawing up of
our present baptismal rituals was not very well
done. There is need for a ritual better adapted
for use with infants, and the desire has long
been expressed for the prebaptismal rites to be

spread out over a period once more for adult
converts, so that they can be helped while they
are under instruction and the rites can take on
the meaning and force they had in ancient times.
This restoration of something like the ancient
preparation for baptism is particularly wanted
in mission territories.

The desire for the reform of our baptismal
rite is now being fulfilled. First, there are the
bilingual rituals, which allow a considerable use
of the vernacular in baptism. The one for this
country, lagging well behind most of the others,
came out in 1961. Secondly, the restoration of the
Easter Vigil was an important step in the renewal of our awareness of baptism. Baptisms
can be given during the Vigil. When they are,
the ceremonies that precede the profession of
faith which comes immediately before the baptism itself can be transferred to the Holy Saturday. Thirdly, on 16 April 1962 a decree was
issued setting forth a new arrangement of the
rite of adult baptism. This splits up the rite into
different stages, so that there are six liturgical
actions before the baptism itself, which comes
as the seventh. The prebaptismal ceremonies
now go step by step with the instruction of the
convert. Some modifications are also introduced
into the ceremonies. The adoption of this new
ritual is at the discretion of the local hierarchies.

They are allowed to have most of it translated into the vernacular and also to make changes in the ceremonies where demanded by local circumstances—it had been found in mission territories that certain ceremonies had unacceptable local meanings. This new ritual is an important step forward in giving the prebaptismal ceremonies a real meaning. It is not regarded as a definitive reform, and further changes are expected. No doubt, some improvements will be made too in the ritual for the baptism of infants.

Against the historical background that has been sketched, let us now consider our present rite for infant baptism.

The rite falls into three parts. The first part may be headed "Acceptance by the Church"; it consists of the ancient rites for the making of a catechumen. "Struggle with Evil and Preparation for Life" is a good heading for the second part, which is made up of ceremonies and prayers from the ancient proximate preparation for baptism that took place during Lent and on Holy Saturday morning. The third part is the celebration of baptism, with a preceding profession of faith and the subsequent symbolic rites of the anointing, the white garment and the lighted candle.

In the first part, then, we find the rites by which in the fourth and fifth centuries a person became a catechumen and began the long remote preparation for baptism. The opening questions and answers are the remnant of the preliminary enquiry and of the first instruction in the rudiments of the Faith. Then come the ceremonies of admission: the exsufflation or the blowing gently into the face of the child to drive away the devil; the imprinting of the sign of the cross on the forehead and breast; the laying on of the hands as a mark of blessing and protection; and lastly the blessing and giving of the salt.

The origin of the rite with the salt is probably the custom of giving salt as a gesture of hospitality. The convert was welcomed as a stranger would be welcomed by being offered salt. The Liturgy has given the salt various meanings. It is a first food given to those preparing for baptism to help them wait patiently for the perfect heavenly food of the Eucharist. Again, salt gives things flavour and preserves them; so it is a symbol of wisdom coming from God which gives us a sense of the things of God and preserves us from the corruption of the world. The symbolism is somewhat artificial, and it is doubtful whether it can ever be made to mean much to people today. One wonders if it might not be better to drop the rite, since there is no biblical tradition behind it.

This first part of the baptismal rite ends with the prayer *Deus Patrum* ("God of our fathers"), which looks forward to baptism and the Eucharist.

In its second part the rite of infant baptism has kept very little from the ancient scrutinies; the rite for adults has retained more. For infants, the single exorcism, the signing of the forehead and the imposition of hands, which now open the second part of the rite, are all that is left of the first six scrutinies. But we might in any case be puzzled about the meaning for infants of this group of ceremonies which is principally an exorcising of the candidate. To understand what is meant we must remember that it is not a question of any extraordinary diabolical influence, like possession. Such an influence involving a departure from the ordinary course of nature is what we first think of when exorcism is mentioned today. It is not envisaged here. The exorcisms over the unbaptized are an expression of the Church's belief that the unredeemed world, as unredeemed, is subject to Satan. The first order of things went wrong through sin, and the leader of the sinful order is Satan. We must be rescued from it by Christ. The dominion of Satan over the child is the lack of grace. Moreover, if the child is not brought within the Church by baptism, it will be without the normal aids God intended for its personal struggle with evil during its growing up. The prayers were originally written for adults and have in mind the difficulties of the period of instruction and growth in the Faith that preceded their baptism. Although infants are rescued immediately from Satan's dominion by the grace of baptism, a period of instruction and growth follows in which they must personally accept their baptismal grace. These exorcisms may be referred to this subsequent struggle, to which they are committed by their baptism as infants. After all, it is part of their initiation, since it precedes their confirmation and their first Holy Communion, and it is only by these sacraments that Christian initiation is completed.

When the first group of ceremonies in the second part of the infant rite is finished, the priest leads the infant into the church with the words, "Come into the temple of God, that your lot may be with Christ in life eternal." This rite is a late addition coming from the thirteenth century. It does not make much sense at this point. In the early Church, once a person was a catechumen he could take some part in the services in the church, but only baptism gave full membership of the worshipping community. To put a symbolic entry into the church in the middle of the preparatory rites is to deprive it of any clear meaning. It could perhaps be moved to the end of the first part of the rite, which corresponds to the making of a catechumen.

The entry into the church is followed by the rites that originally took place on the morning of Holy Saturday. The Creed and the Our Father are said. This is the old *redditio* or giving back of the Creed and the Lord's Prayer, although since the priest says it with the godparents it can be seen as a merging of the *traditio* or handing over and the *redditio* or giving back. Next comes a final exorcism. After this the priest touches the ears and nose of the infant with his thumb wet with saliva, saying: "*Ephpheta*, which is, Be you open to the sweet fragrance about you. As for you, evil spirit, get you gone; for God's judgement is upon you." This is followed by the renunciation of Satan, and this second part concludes with the anointing of the breast and shoulders with the oil of catechumens.

Originally the *Ephpheta* ceremony was part of the anointing and it was done with the oil of catechumens. In our present rite the anointing has been cut in two by the renunciation of Satan, and saliva has replaced oil in touching the ears and nostrils. The use of saliva appears to be a revival of a pagan custom. It was the practice in Rome to smear the eyes, ears and nostrils of newly-born children with saliva as a protection against evil spirits. This custom came into the Liturgy in the fifth or sixth century, chiefly because of the analogy with the miracle in which Christ cured the deaf-mute by using saliva and the word *Ephpheta*. (Mark 7.31–7.) The use of saliva in performing the ceremony may now be dropped at the discretion of the celebrant.

The ancient rite of renouncing Satan needs no comment, except to say that the pomps of the devil meant the manifestations of pagan worship, particularly processions and games, which the Christians were tempted to attend. In the East the renunciation of Satan is followed by a rite expressing adherence to Christ, a rite unknown in the West.

The meaning of the anointing with the oil of catechumens is to be found in the prayer *Deus incrementorum* with which it is blessed on Maundy Thursday. (See the *Pontificale Romanum*.) The prayer indicates that the oil is destined for those approaching baptism. It asks that the last traces of the evil spirits and their wickedness may be removed. The oil is seen as giving strength. The Fathers compared this anointing with the anointing of athletes customary in ancient times. The candidate is prepared by it for the Christian combat that begins in baptism.

After the anointing the baptism itself takes place. It is immediately preceded by a profession of faith in the form of questions and answers. This profession of faith was, as we have seen, formerly at the very centre of the rite in the place now occupied by the baptismal form. Three ceremonies follow the baptism, the anointing, the clothing with a white garment and the giving of a lighted candle. The second two have already been discussed; I shall come back to the anointing later.

The history of the celebration of baptism is complicated, but its very complexity shows how the Church has continually adapted her rites to the changing historical situation. The guiding force behind the changes has been the pastoral concern of the Church. We should not, then, be surprised or disturbed to find that the very different conditions of our own time are causing the Church to overhaul her ritual once more.

DEATH AND RESURRECTION

W̲HAT does baptism do for the person baptized? The previous chapters have already given much that answers this question. It was hardly possible to study the symbolism of baptism and the history of its celebration without saying much about its purpose and effects. After all, the symbols and the celebration as a whole are intended to express what baptism does. But there is room for a further treatment of this, which will give the results of theological reflection on the data so far presented.

A suitable starting-point is the relation between baptism and faith. The Fathers called baptism the sacrament of faith, and the Council of Trent in the sixteenth century made the expression its own. (See Denzinger, 799.) Even today the close connection between baptism and faith emerges pretty clearly from the baptismal rite. There are the opening question and answer: "What do you ask of the Church of God?" "Faith." ("The Faith" would be a better translation of the answer, because what the prospective catechumen is here asking from the Church is not so much the inner virtue of faith as the object of faith. In other words, he wants to be taught the beliefs of Christians and especially their rule of conduct. Hence he is given for his guidance the two commandments of love.) Then, just before the baptism itself is a solemn profession of faith in the form of an interrogatory creed. Coming immediately afterwards, baptism ratifies that act of faith. Yet, in the first centuries, when adult baptism was the norm, the bond between baptism and faith was even more strikingly evident. People were baptized *by* the Creed, inasmuch as their profession of faith in answer to the questions of the priest was part of the essential action of baptism. Baptism was constituted by the immersion and the profession of faith; there was no formula of baptizing said by the priest. Baptism was truly the sacrament of faith. The Church had prepared the candidate for baptism by instructing him in the Faith. She now called upon him to declare his acceptance of that faith. He did so in taking part in a sacramental rite that ratified and sealed his faith and established him as a member of the community of believers.

To understand the place of faith in baptism it is necessary to have some idea of the part played by faith in the sacraments generally. All the sacraments are signs of faith, expressions of the faith of the Church.

It is a popular distortion of the sacraments to see them as things. But the sacraments are not things but human actions. The sacraments are signs, but the sacramental sign is not a thing but an external expression in word and gesture of a spiritual activity. The sacrament is the embodiment in symbol of the interior and spiritual activity of the Church. Certainly, things are made use of in the symbolic actions, but the sacrament lies in their use, not in the things themselves. In brief, the sacraments are symbolic actions of the Church. In them the Church embodies and expresses her faith and worship. They are actions of Christ as well, with an efficacy from him. But they are actions of Christ in so far as they are the actions of the Church, his body. Imbued with the power of Christ, they remain actions which the Church does to express her faith and worship.

All the sacraments rest upon the faith of the Church because they are by their nature expressions of that faith. Man's symbolic actions spring from his spiritual consciousness. It is his spiritual consciousness that gives meaning to the external action and the spoken word. Without this inner spiritual awareness and intention no action done by a man would properly be a

symbol. The spiritual consciousness from which
the sacraments spring and which constitutes
them as symbols is the faith of the Church. So,
the faith of the Church enters into the structure
of the sacraments. It is the mind or consciousness
of the Church, her common faith, that gives the
sacraments their meaning and makes them the
symbolic actions of a believing and worshipping
community. This mind of the Church is the
mind of Christ. He formed it and keeps it true
to himself by the Holy Spirit. He, too, established the sacraments as expressions of his mind
and signs of the faith of the Church. The sacraments are not indeed spontaneous signs created
for the nonce, but institutional signs that we
must accept before they become our own. They
do presuppose, however, the faith of the Church;
without this they could exist, because it alone
gives them their meaning. They are signs of
faith.

The sacraments are actions of the Church.
They are hers, and they can exist only when
supported by her faith. The individual minister
and recipient can carry out a true sacrament
only if they join themselves to the Church and
her faith. The minimum link with the faith of
the Church is the intention in doing the action
of doing what the Church does. This minimum
can be present without any personal faith in

minister or recipient. But it is only a minimum, and although it secures the validity of the sacraments, it is anomalous. It is normal for a sacrament to express the personal faith of both minister and recipient. It is particularly important that a sacrament should express the faith of the recipient, because otherwise it remains unfruitful. The faith or lack of faith and the holiness or lack of holiness in the minister do not affect the power with which a sacrament sanctifies the recipient. But the recipient's own faith, together with the other dispositions that flow from faith but vary with the different sacraments, is necessary for the fruitfulness of the sacrament. Further than that, the measure in which it bears fruit is in proportion to the response of the recipient.

People often separate our response from the sacraments unduly, as if what we did in receiving a sacrament was altogether outside the sacrament, serving simply as a preliminary condition. It is true that in the sacraments God's gift through Christ comes first and is there independently of our response. This is what we mean by the objective efficacy of the sacraments; we do not give them their power—that comes from Christ. But our response is essential to a fruitful sacrament and is part of the meaning of every sacrament as a symbolic action. Without our personal response a sacrament loses its full mean-

ing. It is partly falsified, and we act a lie. Our
response is not outside the sacrament but enters
into it, because it is expressed by the sacrament.
The celebration of a sacrament is an expression
of Christ's gift to us and of the faith of the
Church, but it is designed as the expression of
the recipient's personal faith as well.

Can we analyse the part played by the recipient's response more closely? A person approaching the sacraments must already have the
beginnings of a response to God's gift. Certain
dispositions, the basic one being faith, are required before the sacrament is actually received.
There must be an initial movement towards the
encounter with Christ that is going to be
achieved in the sacrament. This first, imperfect
movement allows contact to be established between Christ and the person, so that Christ can
act upon him and give grace. As I have said, the
sacraments are not things, but meaningful
human actions. They are symbolic actions that
get their meaning from faith. Now, to cause
grace in us, the sacraments must make contact
with us; there must be some bond between us
and the symbolic action. It is not enough for this
contact to be a bodily contact. The sacraments
are signs; they cause as signs; they must make
contact as signs. How do they do so? Through
the faith and devotion, the personal response of

the recipient. By the initial faith of the recipient, contact is established on the spiritual level between him and the action of Christ in the sacrament. Hence the initial response with which the person approaches the sacrament makes it possible for the sacrament to exert its power.

When the sacraments are approached in this way their celebration becomes an expression of our longing for grace and our will to encounter Christ. And in the sacrament this encounter with Christ takes place, so that the sacrament becomes an expression of the encounter achieved between the recipient and Christ. It is the sacrament itself that brings our response to full maturity. The sacraments give grace by the power of Christ, but they do so only by creating a full response in us. Sanctifying grace is never given to an adult except in an act of charity. God never pours grace into an adult without a free response being actually involved in the bestowal. The sacraments give grace by bringing the initial movement to its fullness in a personal act of love by which we accept justification or welcome a deepening of our existing friendship. The sacraments are a personal encounter with Christ. They do not simply express our union with Christ, but by expressing it in a symbol to which Christ promised his presence they bring it to a new intensity, just as our affection for another is intensified by actual bodily encounter. The sacraments stand out from the rest of our Christian life as privileged expressions of our union with Christ, which give it a new intensity by embodying it in a symbolic action to which Christ attached his power.

This long digression about the sacraments in general was, I felt, necessary if the relation of baptism to faith was to be properly understood. Does baptism give faith or presuppose faith? The question comes up frequently and some obscurity evidently surrounds it. This is due partly to the fact that baptism nearly always means infant baptism, and partly to the general neglect of the part that belongs to the recipient in a sacramental celebration. How, then, do the adult's faith and the sacramental action meet so as to make a fruitful sacrament of faith?

Baptism undoubtedly presupposes some faith. The person asking to become a catechumen would at least have had an attraction towards the Faith, an attraction due to the work of grace. This first stirring of faith would have been strengthened by the three years of instruction and particularly the last intensive period of proximate preparation, which included, it will be remembered, the handing over and the giving back of the Creed. By Easter Night the candidate would have advanced some way in faith. By his personal striving for God, a striving caused by God's actual graces, he would, in all probability, have reached the virtue of faith and indeed the state of grace; for we can readily suppose an irrevocable commitment to God occurring before the baptism itself. But at all events faith before baptism remained imperfect. It was so, not primarily by lack of subjective earnestness, but by lack of the stability and qualitative enrichment given only by sacramental encounter with Christ. At the same time, without some initial faith, the sacrament would have been unfruitful.

If baptism presupposes some faith, it also gives faith. Not by pouring the gift of faith into an unresponsive subject but by bringing the person's initial faith to maturity in a symbolic action that expresses it and at the same time perfects it through the power of Christ. All the sacraments express and deepen our faith in this way. But baptism is the sacrament of faith in a special way, because it is the first public profession of faith by the candidate in which he irrevocably commits himself to Christ and accepts his message, and his solemn acceptance by the Church as a believer. Baptism makes him one of the faithful, gives him membership of the Church, the community of believers. The ceremonies of the handing over and giving back of the Creed were a kind of rehearsal for the profession of faith that constituted baptism itself.

All this is still true of the unbaptized adult convert. An initial faith must precede the sacrament, and normally the person has advanced a fair way in the Faith before baptism. Baptism perfects and confirms that faith, and joins the convert to the community of believers. Admittedly, we now use a baptismal form instead of the profession of faith in the action of baptizing, but the profession of faith still immediately precedes the actual baptism and thus indicates that baptism is of its very nature a profession of faith for the recipient.

But what about infant baptism? Is it still the sacrament of faith? Yes; but with the differences called for by the different condition of the recipient. Since the infant is incapable of a personal response, God does with it what he never does with an adult: treats it passively. The infant is given in baptism all the permanent gifts involved in the state of grace, including the virtue of faith. The virtue of faith comes for the first time without any previous imperfect faith. The Church, however, will not baptize an infant unless someone undertakes to educate it as a Catholic; in other words, unless there is some assurance that the child will be led to a personal act of faith in Christ. Baptism here is still ordered by its dynamism to the act of faith. Moreover, it is the faith of the Church that makes infant baptism possible. In the symbolic action of baptism the infant is carried, as it were, by the faith of the Church. It is only because the believing community takes the infant as its own, surrounds it with signs of faith and expresses the Faith on its behalf that its baptism becomes a meaningful rite, an intelligible expression of faith in Christ and in the sanctifying presence of his sanctifying power.

To turn back for a moment to the baptism of adults. I have described baptism as a profession of faith, but I must hasten to add that this is no mere intellectual acceptance of what Christ said. Christian faith is that, but much more as well. We proclaim our faith to express our commitment to Christ. In baptism we take our stand with Christ against the powers of darkness. This is beautifully expressed in the rite of adherence to Christ that immediately follows the renunciation of Satan in the Eastern Churches. Baptism, then, is a total commitment to Christ, but we must recognize that this commitment can be achieved only in answer to the call of Christ. The initiative of Christ is shown in the preparatory rites where the signings of the cross on the person indicate that Christ is gradually taking possession of him and making him his own. The

Fathers expressed the commitment involved in baptism by speaking of baptism as a contract or pact. This evokes the thought that baptism makes us members of the New Covenant. The sign of the Old Covenant was circumcision; Paul calls baptism Christ's circumcision: "In him you have been circumcised with a circumcision that was not man's handiwork. It was effected, not by despoiling the natural body, but by Christ's circumcision; you, by baptism, have been united with his burial, united, too, with his resurrection, through your faith in that exercise of power by which God raised him from the dead." (Col. 2.11–12.) Our covenant with God is like a pact in that we pledge our faith and undertake obligations; but it is unlike ordinary pacts in depending entirely on the free initiative of God's love. The contractual idea of baptism is strongly present in the renewal of baptismal promises on Easter Night and at missions.

One of the reasons why baptism is the sacrament of faith is that it joins us to the Church, the community of believers. Baptism, then, is our entry into the Church. By it we are made members of the Church of Christ.

Baptism is not a private affair between the individual and God but a matter that concerns the community. This was very clear in earlier centuries. The convert had to come to the representatives of the Church and get himself accepted as a catechumen, and for this he needed the recommendation of a member of the community. His preparation for baptism was under direction, and the community took part in the scrutinies which marked its later stages. Baptism was celebrated in common on Easter Night, and the community was there to welcome its new members.

It is still true that baptism is a community affair. It is essential to baptism to be such. The baptism of an infant is not just a family affair. It is the acceptance of a new member into the parochial community, which is the Church as present in a particular place. Through its minister the community joins a person to itself. Although the community is always present in the person of the minister and in the relatives of the child, it is fitting that others should take part in order to mark better the significance of the event.

Baptism is the cause of our membership of the Church. The unbaptized who sincerely seek God's will are related to the Church, belong to her in a certain sense, by that desire for membership which is implicit in their readiness to do whatever God wants. Just as we speak of baptism of desire, so we can speak of membership of the Church by desire; for in fact the two come to the same thing. What is meant is that if any person sincerely follows his conscience he will be brought to the love of God through the working of God's grace within him. This love of God implies a willingness to do God's will in all things; such a general willingness embraces baptism and membership of the Church, though the person remains unaware that these are God's will. All the same, we do not refer to the unbaptized, however sincere, as baptized, nor can we call them members of the Church. Although they can be saved by their love of God, they have not been incorporated into the sacramental community of the Church and they are cut off from the privileges of membership. Baptism opens the way to the other sacraments; only the baptized can receive them. Only the baptized, too, can take part in the public worship of the Church as members of the assembly that offers it. Nowadays others can be present and join spiritually in what is going on. But they do not form part of the assembly that carries out the sacramental celebration and is the bearer of the mystery that is made present. Baptism alone aggregates us to the community that actively celebrates the worship offered by Christ in his mystical body.

But if baptism causes our membership of the Church, it does so as an expression of our faith

and union with the Church. For that reason it
can be partially frustrated in its effects by a
defect in that faith or union. When baptism is
given outside the visible unity of the Catholic
Church, it still unites the baptized persons organically to the Church. Anyone who is baptized
belongs to the Church in a way that the unbaptized do not. All the baptized are our brothers in
the Church. But if they are outside the visible
unity of the Church, separated from us in faith
and communion, they do not enjoy full membership. The union with the Church given by their
baptism cannot have its full effect. They are
deprived of some of the privileges of membership, and their Christian life is in an anomalous
situation. Only the baptized who profess the
true faith and are within the visible unity of the
Catholic Church are in the full sense members
of Christ's Church. Nevertheless, we must not
forget our union with our separated brothers;
the bond that unites us through our common
baptism is deeper and stronger than what divides
us.

In becoming a member of the Church by baptism we are not just joining a society of men. The
Church is no ordinary society; it is the Body
of Christ. To join the Church is to be made one
with Christ; for the Church and all the members of the Church achieve a kind of identity

with Christ. This at once confronts us with the mystery of our redemption by Christ. There is a temptation to think of the work of atonement as something which Christ did in our stead, so that all we do is to benefit from it. That is not so. Christ acted as our representative. He did what we could not do alone. But he acted as our leader, opening for us the way along which we must follow him. What took place in Christ when he died and rose again must take place in us too. We do not become Christians simply by accepting the teaching of Christ and receiving from him graces that he merited in a redemptive work in which we have no part. We become Christians only by sharing in the redemptive work itself. We have to relive in our own experience the death and resurrection of Christ. Our identification with Christ is the reproduction in ourselves of what he underwent. We, as sinners, could not achieve a death and resurrection of ourselves. But Christ has gone before us, and his death and resurrection is the power by which we die and rise again. In brief, we die with Christ and rise again with him.

Since baptism is our incorporation into Christ, our first identification with Christ, it is by baptism that we first die with Christ and rise again with him. This is one of the main themes in the Pauline theology of baptism. In the Epistle

4

to the Romans he writes: "You know well enough that we who were taken up into Christ by baptism have been taken up, all of us, into his death. In our baptism, we have been buried with him, died like him, that so, just as Christ was raised up by his Father's power from the dead, we too might live and move in a new kind of existence. We have to be closely fitted into the pattern of his resurrection, as we have been into the pattern of his death." (Rom. 6.3–5.) This passage forcefully states the relation of baptism to the death and burial of Christ, but it is less clear about the relation of baptism to the Resurrection. But St. Paul had developed his thought by the time he wrote the passage I have already quoted from Colossians: "You, by baptism, have been united with his burial, united, too, with his resurrection, through your faith in that exercise of power by which God raised him from the dead." (Col. 2.12.) Baptism unites us to Christ's resurrection as it unites us to his death. In the Epistle to the Ephesians, Paul goes so far as to see us sharing the ascension and enthronement of Christ: "How rich God is in mercy, with what an excess of love he loved us! Our sins had made dead men of us, and he, in giving life to Christ, gave life to us too; it is his grace that has saved you; raised us up too, enthroned us too above the heavens, in Christ Jesus." (Eph. 2.4–6.) Our

baptism unites us to Christ in glory. We have
undergone that same process that led Christ
through the humiliation of Calvary to his exaltation at the right hand of his Father.

That baptism is a death and resurrection is
driven home with emphasis by the symbolism it
uses, as we saw in the first chapter. There is no
need to delay over the fact. But to understand
what is meant by our baptismal death and resurrection, it is necessary to consider briefly the
nature of Christ's redemptive activity.

Man separated himself from God by sin. Sin
destroyed his friendship with God. He lost the
presence of God, the intimacy and personal relation with God, which was the purpose for
which God had created him. But sin had also
wider repercussions. It was the disruption of
God's order in the world. Man lost the gifts that
gave harmony to his complex nature and which
would have ensured the tranquil development
of the human race on earth. They were lost because they were rooted in the grace of God's
friendship and went with it. Sinful man was in
a state of inner conflict, unable to follow the
dictates of his better self. He was subject to
suffering and distress in all their many forms.
Above all, death was now his lot. There is an
absurdity about death. It is the break-up of
man's personality, the loss by the soul of its

medium of contact with the rest of reality and
a cessation in the activity and development of
human life. The soul survives but confined
within itself in an empty existence. In its un-
intelligibility death is a visible image of sin as
it is its result. Death may also be taken as a sign
of the power of the Evil One. By his sin man put
himself into the hands of Satan. Satan had already rebelled against God. He entrapped man
into his kingdom of darkness. Man had been
created as the lord of this visible creation. He
became a slave of Satan, the ruler of this present
darkness. As St. John puts it: "The whole world
about us lies in the power of the Evil One."
(1 John. 5.19.) Such was the state of man as left
by sin, a state in which sin continued to multiply
and death reigned supreme.

But God intended to save man. How did he
do so? "God so loved the world, that he gave up
his only-begotten Son, so that those who believe
in him may not perish, but have eternal life.
When God sent his Son into the world, it was
not to reject the world, but so that the world
might find salvation through him." (John
3.16–17.) That is St. John's statement. This is
how Paul puts it: "Then God sent out his Son
on a mission to us. He took birth from a woman,
took birth as a subject of the law, so as to ransom
those who were subject to the law, and make us

sons by adoption." (Gal. 4.4–5.) God sent his
Son "into the world", sent him as "subject to
the law". In other words, the Son came into this
sinful world and joined himself to the sinful
human race. Now, Christ, God the Son made
man, could not share the guilt of sin. He was
completely free from sin and from that disorder
within us that is incompatible with complete
innocence. But he accepted our human nature
in the condition in which it had been left by
sin, subject to suffering and death. He entered
into our human situation that was affected by
sin, entangled in the consequences of sin and
subject to the attacks of Satan. God sent his Son,
Paul tells us, "in the fashion of our guilty nature,
to make amends for our guilt" (Rom. 8.3); and
even more strongly, "Christ never knew sin, and
God made him into sin for us, so that in him
we might be turned into the holiness of God."
(2 Cor. 5.21.)

The Incarnation, then, involved a self-abasement by the Son. Here again we can turn to
Paul. "He dispossessed himself, and took the
nature of a slave, fashioned in the likeness of
men, and presenting himself to us in human
form; and then he lowered his own dignity,
accepted an obedience which brought him to
death, death on a cross." (Phil. 2.7–8.) This dis-
possession meant that the Son accepted a distance

from the Father. This separation could be realized only in his human nature, but let us beware of making that mean that it was unreal. God the Son died on the Cross; he died only according to his human nature; but that does not mean that God the Son did not really die. The Hypostatic Union means that what happened in Christ's human nature happened to God the Son. The Son, I repeat, accepted a distance from the Father. In becoming man in a sinful human race, he entered a situation where he was without the glory, that is, the nearness to God, that was his due as Son. As man he was not fully penetrated with the divine holiness; the human nature he assumed was partly opaque to it.

So, Christ accepted a solidarity with sinful mankind. But how did that lead to our redemption? It did so, because Christ, being sinless and completely united to the Father's will by his loving obedience, gave our state a new meaning. Instead of being the expression of sin, it became the expression of sacrificial love. He lived out our state to its end, death, and in his death it was destroyed. His death called down the saving action of the Father by which he rescued Christ from death, established him as the first-fruits of a new order, a new creation, and exalted him to his full glory as Son. In his death Christ passed from this world of sin and death to the glory of the Resurrection. We have to make the same passage in union with him.

From its outset Christ's life was a life of utter surrender to his Father's will. We read in John: "It is the will of him who sent me, not my own will, that I have come down from heaven to do." (John 6.38.) This unswerving fidelity inevitably led him into conflict with the powers of evil that ruled the world. "In him there was life, and that life was the light of men. And the light shines in darkness, a darkness which was not able to master it." (John 1.4–5). The powers of darkness gathered around him. The Gospels record the growing hostility of the Jewish leaders that eventually led to his death. But behind these was a greater force. John makes that clear when he puts these words into the mouth of Christ: "If God were your Father, you would love me, for I proceeded and came forth from God; I came not of my own accord, but he sent me. Why do you not understand what I say? It is because you cannot bear to hear my word. You are of your father the devil, and your will is to do your father's desires. He was a murderer from the beginning, and has nothing to do with the truth, because there is no truth in him." (John 8.42–4 —Revised Standard Version.) As John put it in his First Epistle, "The reason the Son of God

appeared was to destroy the works of the devil."
(1 John 3.8.) The Synoptic Gospels present us
with the same understanding of Christ's mission.
In their accounts, the temptations in the desert
immediately follow the baptism of Christ. Christ
begins his ministry by confronting the devil. Behind the accounts is a contrasting parallel between Christ and Adam. Christ is the new Adam,
who successfully resists the tempter to whom the
first Adam had succumbed. During his public
ministry Christ cast out devils many times, and
the prominence given to this work of expulsion
shows its great significance. The casting out of
devils showed that Christ had come to overthrow
the kingdom of Satan and thus bring the kingdom of God. In the words of Christ himself:
"But if, when I cast out devils, I do it through
the Spirit of God, then it must be that the kingdom of God has already appeared among you."
(Matt. 12.28.)

Surrounded by an increasingly ominous darkness, Christ carried out his Father's will. He
preached the message of salvation and the coming
of the Kingdom. He prepared for his death,
which he knew was to come. He yearned for it
as his way back to the Father, his Passover or
passing from this world of darkness and sin to
the new order of light and glory. Meanwhile he
began to form his Church, the new People of

God which would result from his death and resurrection—would, as the Fathers said, come forth as a new Eve from his side as he hung on the Cross.

His death eventually came. We can say of Christ's death what was said of all death in the Book of Wisdom: "God made not death: neither hath he pleasure in the destruction of the living." (Wisd. of Sol. 1.13—Douay Version.) His death was a murder, the result of the sinful intrigues of the Jews and the achievement through them of the will of Satan. But in putting Christ to death the rulers of this world of darkness made a mistake. They did not know God's secret, his saving plan. Paul said: "What we make known is the wisdom of God, his secret, kept hidden till now; so, before the ages, God had decreed, reserving glory for us. (None of the rulers of this world could read his secret, or they would not have crucified him to whom all glory belongs.)" (1 Cor. 2.7–8.) By dying Christ changed the meaning of death and made it the gateway to life. Death had been the visible expression of man's sin. It represented the absurdity of man's rebellion against God, the self-destructive nature of his self-seeking refusal to obey. Christ, however, died freely out of obedience to his Father's will. His death was the lowest point in the self-abasement to which his Father had sent him. His death became an act of sacrificial surrender to his Father. It was an expression of his obedient love of the Father and of his redemptive love for mankind. Death, which had been the embodiment of man's sin, became in Christ the embodiment of love. Here was the opposite of man's disobedient self-seeking; the reality that comes to expression in Christ's death is a loving self-surrender.

The outcome of such a death could not but be different. "Father, into thy hands I commend my spirit." (Luke 23.46.) The cry of Christ was answered. With an act of love the Father reached down from heaven and took his Son into his embrace. The death of Christ became the meeting-point of God's love and the sinful world. The Father raised Christ from the dead and exalted him in glory as Lord. He now had all the glory due to him as Son. The love of the Father for the Son by which he raised him from the dead was sealed in the gift of the Spirit. The Spirit, the pledge and bond of love, now fully penetrated the human nature of Christ and made it diaphanous to the divine holiness.

In Christ a new order, a new creation, was established. Men are invited to share in the life and glory of the risen Christ. In his death Christ died to this order and entered a new. Men must undergo the same process of dying to this order and entering the new order of the Resurrection. But they can do so only by the power of Christ's own death and resurrection. The reason is that the historical drama of Christ's death and resurrection, made permanent by the present glory of the living Christ, was intended by God as a definitive expression of his will to save man. As we express our mind and will by words and gestures, so God expressed his plan and will to save man in the events of Christ. What happened in Christ is a great symbol formed of the stuff of history, a symbol of God's saving love. And expression of God's will brings about what it expresses, just as Christ's mere command healed the sick. We are saved by God's will as expressed in the events of Christ, which culminated and reached eternal permanence in his exaltation to the right hand of the Father.

We are put in touch with the mystery of Christ by commemorating it symbolically in the sacraments. The symbolism of the sacraments recalls the events of Christ, in particular his death and resurrection. By recalling the mystery of Christ for us, the sacraments bring to bear upon us the power of God's saving love as expressed in Christ. But Christ is still living and the sacraments are his doing still. Through the activity of the Church his body, Christ, in these symbolic commemorations of his work, continues to express that redemptive love of his which was given its primordial expression in the drama of Calvary. So, the sacraments are an encounter with the living Christ. God's gift comes to us from his hands, and we are able to insert our response into his own loving surrender, which has never ceased. We die and rise again by the power of Christ's own death and resurrection. But it is in union with the living Christ that we do so. We die with Christ—that is, in loving union with him—and we rise with him to share his present glory.

All this is true of all the sacraments, because our dying and rising with Christ is not something that happens completely all at once. Our whole Christian life is a process of dying and rising with Christ, since only gradually do we receive the fullness of our redemption. Each sacrament, then, in its own way deepens our death in Christ and intensifies our union with his risen life. In a very special sense, however, baptism is the sacrament of our dying and rising with Christ. The reason is that in it we achieve the essential transition from the old order to the new. The baptized essentially belong to the new order of the Resurrection. They have entered a new existence and possess eternal life. They have passed from darkness to light, from slavery to freedom, from the kingdom of Satan to the kingdom of Christ. The transition is not yet complete, but what remains to be done is growth whereas baptism was the birth.

What are the implications of our baptismal death and resurrection? The death meant for us the destruction of sin and release from the power of Satan. Unlike Christ, the Son of God by nature, we came into this sinful world without any title of our own to grace. Children of Adam, we were involved in his downfall. We were born deprived of grace, cut off from God by original sin. Our baptismal death was the destruction of that state of sin. If we came to baptism as adults after having further entangled ourselves in our sinful situation by personal sins, the sacrament will have taken away all those personal sins as well. Baptism takes away all sin, both original and personal. In taking away sin, baptism freed us from the slavery of Satan. By sin we were entrapped in the order of which Satan is the ruler. What has been said about Christ and Satan explains the constant references to Satan in the preparatory rites of baptism, the way he is repeatedly driven off until the final renunciation of him and his works by the candidate, which comes just before the baptism itself.

But our death to sin is not completed when we receive baptism. The consequences of sin are not entirely removed. The disorder within ourselves is counteracted but not extinguished. We have to struggle against it and complete our baptismal death by our personal efforts, although for these we can draw on the strength of Christ, given to us particularly in the other sacraments. We have still to undergo physical death. But the death of a Christian is different in meaning from the death of a sinner. It is a death linked to Christ's death and has a similar meaning. No longer an expression of sin, it is an expression of our final surrender in love to God and the point where we pass into a closer embrace of his love. Our physical death is the final accomplishment of what we undertake when we commit ourselves to Christ in baptism, accepting as we do then to go down with him into the waters of death.

But we do not have to wait until our physical death before we begin to share Christ's resurrection. Already at baptism we rise with Christ. By this resurrection we come alive with the life of Christ. We enjoy his life and share his glory. We have it yet only in part and largely in a hidden fashion. It has to grow and gradually penetrate our whole being. It will reach its fullness only after death, and even then it will be further perfected in the resurrection of the body. Still, after baptism it is there, and we live and move in a new existence. It is the life of grace. But what does that mean?

The life of grace is often explained as if it were an impersonal thing. The impression is given of the infusion of some higher kind of biological life that can be lived below the personal level. But the life of grace is an intensely personal life. It is a new personal relation with God. We could not live in such personal intimacy with God unless he transformed our nature and gave it new powers. But this new, supernatural equipping of our nature is only to make possible a life that has to be lived on the personal level. It is our entry into the personal life of the Godhead.

As personal, God is a Trinity, and so our life of grace is a share in the life of the Trinity and involves a personal relation with each of the persons of the Trinity. We share this life by union with Christ, the Son of God. We have therefore this life as sons. We possess the divine life as sons in the Son, sharing his relation to the Father and the Spirit.

Our personal relation to the Father is that of sons. Baptism makes us adopted sons of the Father. We can look to him as Father; for we are in reality his sons, though only by sharing the sonship of the Son. The personal intimacy of a

son to his father is ours with the first person of
the Trinity. He is the ultimate source of our
life, and we participate in the knowledge and
love that unite Father and Son in the life of the
Trinity.

Our personal relation to the Son is that of
brothers. He is the model of our life of grace,
the pattern after whom we are formed when we
are given a share in the divine life. Since he took
our nature and thus put himself on an equality
with us we can call him our brother. We are
joined to him, so that it is his life we possess, his
relation to the Father we share. Our personal intimacy with him must be expressed in terms of
identity, though our distinct personality is not
absorbed.

The union of Father and Son in the life of the
Trinity is sealed by the Spirit. The Spirit is the
mutual Gift with which they pledge their love.
If the Son is Word or Thought, the Spirit is
Love, and so the Spirit is the bond of union.
Since we enter the union between Father and
Son, we receive the Spirit as Gift. Father and
Son give us the Spirit, and by the Spirit in the
Son we are drawn to the Father. The Spirit is
our indwelling Guest, and it is because we have
received the Spirit as Gift that the Father and
Son are present with us. Our personal relation
to the Spirit leads us to welcome him as the

Guest that comes as the pledge of love from Father and Son, and who by making his dwelling within us joins us to Christ as our brother and leads us as sons to the Father.

Thus, the life of grace is a deeply personal reality. The three persons of the Trinity give themselves in us and invite us to a new, personal relation with themselves. Our baptismal regeneration brings us into an intimate union with each of the three persons. For that reason it is most appropriate that the baptismal form is trinitarian. It runs: "I baptize thee in the name of the Father and of the Son and of the Holy Ghost." Part of its meaning is that baptism consecrates the person to the Trinity. By consecration I do not mean simply the dedicating of the person to the Trinity by an act of will. The consecration is constitutive of a new state of existence. Our being and our life are transformed, and we are made part of that community of love which unites Father, Son and Holy Spirit. We enter this community by taking our place with God the Son as sons in him. We become sons of God the Father, related to him in his only-begotten Son and joined to both by the Spirit. This is the grace given by baptism. It is a share in the life of the risen Christ, the bestowal of adopted sonship and the gift of the Spirit.

Our personal union with Christ, I have just said, must be expressed in terms of identity. It is his life as incarnate Son that we all share when we become adopted sons. This must give depth to what has already been said on baptism as our entry into the Church. The Church is the body of Christ, and when we entered the Church by baptism we were organically united into one body with our fellow members, a body in which we share the one life of Christ. "We too, all of us," says St. Paul, "have been baptized into a single body by the power of a single Spirit, Jews and Greeks, slaves and free men alike." (1 Cor. 12.13.) Our Christian life is a communion with one another in Christ. There is no such thing as an isolated Christian; it is a contradiction in terms. We have our Christian life as the branches of a vine in the one vine, as organs and members of the one body. By baptism each of us is identified with the glorified Christ, so that we live with his risen life. We therefore become one with one another by our common identity with Christ.

We must never forget, however, that our union with Christ is a personal union. If we use terms of identity it is to express the strength and closeness of the union, not to reduce it to the impersonal level. There is a danger of understanding the theme of the body of Christ in an impersonal way, almost as though the Church really were the same as a biological organism. It is well, then, to remember that our union with Christ is expressed in terms of another theme, the theme of the Church as the bride of Christ. The New Testament applies the idea of the bridal union between God and his chosen people to the union between Christ and his Church. In expounding this idea Paul sees baptism as a marriage rite by which Christ prepared the Church to be his spotless bride: "You who are husbands must shew love to your wives, as Christ shewed love to the Church when he gave himself up on its behalf. He would hallow it, purify it by bathing it in the water to which his word gave life; he would summon it into his own presence, the Church in all its beauty, no stain, no wrinkle, no such disfigurement; it was to be holy, it was to be spotless." (Eph. 5.25–8.)

When using this theme of the Church as a whole, the Fathers add an element to it not expressly found in Scripture, though in line with its teaching: the fruitfulness of the union. The Church bears children to Christ. Hence the teaching developed on the Church as Mother. This is found very early—already, in fact, in the second century. It is in connection with this that we have the idea of the baptismal waters as the womb of the Church. It is expressed in the blessing of the font on Easter Night: "May this water, prepared for the rebirth of men, be rendered fruitful by the secret inpouring of his divine power; may a heavenly offspring, conceived in holiness and reborn into a new creation, come forth from the stainless womb of this divine font."

The relation of each individual to Christ may also be expressed in terms of a nuptial union. Its use in Christian spiritual writings should make clear the degree of our personal intimacy with Christ.

Christ lives on in us so that we may go through him to the Father. The life of a Christian is a life directed, as Christ's life was directed, to the Father. This comes to expression in the prayer and worship of the Church. In its basic structure the Liturgy, or public worship of the Church, is directed to the Father through Christ. We do in the Liturgy address Christ and praise him as the incarnate Son. Nevertheless, the ground-plan of the Church's worship is to the Father through Christ in the Spirit. The reason is that Christian prayer is the very prayer *of* Christ rather than prayer *to* Christ. The supreme act of Christian worship is the sacrifice of the Mass, which is the sacrifice offered by Christ to his Father and now offered by the Church with him. The same struc-

ture is found in the rest of our Christian worship.
Our prayer as Christians is the prayer offered by
Christ to his heavenly Father and now prolonged
and continued in us his body. When Christians
pray they do so in virtue of their union with
Christ, the High Priest of the New Testament.

As a Christian, then, each of us is joined to
Christ the Priest. We all share the priesthood of
Christ. Peter said of the baptized: "You are a
chosen race, a royal priesthood, a consecrated
nation, a people God means to have for himself."
(1 Pet. 2.9.) United with Christ the Priest, we
can all enter into the worship he unceasingly
offers. We all, then, have a part in the liturgy
of the Church, which is the worship Christ offers
in his mystical body. It belongs to us all as forming a royal priesthood in Christ. Now, if we consider their spiritual sharing in this worship, all
Christians are equal, whatever their function.
Our spiritual communion with Christ in his
worship depends simply on the intimacy of our
union with him by our degree of holiness; and
that, too, is the measure of its sanctifying effects
on ourselves. From this point of view a simple
layman may be more intimately united to the
sacrifice of Christ than a bishop or priest. But if
we consider the sacramental celebration of that
worship, then there are different grades in the
Church, each with its peculiar functions and

powers. It is the character that establishes a person in a particular grade within the Church.

A character is a permanent and distinctive mark imprinted on the soul and giving the person a particular place in the sacramental structure of the Church. Three sacraments confer a character. They are the three sacraments that establish the person in a particular state in regard to the structure of the Church: baptism, confirmation and holy order. Although the grace given by these sacraments can be lost and regained, the state they confer is definitive and their character is indelible; therefore these sacraments themselves cannot be repeated. Each of the characters is concerned with worship, since the function of the Church as a sacramental organism is worship. A character, then, is, as St. Thomas Aquinas said, a kind of configuration to Christ as Priest. Each of the sacraments conferring a character appoints the person to a particular place in the worship offered to God by the Church as the body of Christ.

That the character of holy order appoints a person to a function in divine worship is too obvious to need comment. All the special powers and functions of the ministerial priesthood are connected with the character conferred on the ordained priest. But baptism and confirmation also appoint people to a place in the liturgy of the Church. Baptism by its character incorporates us into the community that carries out the sacramental celebrations and takes part actively in the worship offered by Christ in his mystical body. All the functions and duties of Christians in regard to the Liturgy and what flows from the Liturgy are based on their baptismal character. The entire sacramental life of a Christian is grounded in his baptismal character; it alone makes possible the reception of the other sacraments. It gives what we may call the common priesthood of all the faithful: the function which every Christian has as a Christian in the Liturgy. The character of confirmation completes that common priesthood, giving it its social and apostolic dimension by constituting the Christian as a witness of Christian realities before the world.

The sacrament of our faith in Christ, which incorporates us into the community of true believers; our death and resurrection in Christ, by which we are consecrated to the Trinity and enter as sons into the life of the Godhead; the sacrament which joins us to Christ the High Priest and gives us a part in his worship: truly, baptism is the beginning of a new life and our transference to a new order of existence. Implicit in it is the programme for Christian living.

"And you, too, must think of yourselves as dead
to sin, and alive with a life that looks towards
God, through Christ Jesus our Lord." (Rom.
6.11.)

ANOINTED WITH THE SPIRIT

CHRIST had promised his apostles to send them the Spirit. According to Luke, this promise was fulfilled on Pentecost Day. We read in the second chapter of the Acts how, "while they were all gathered together in unity of purpose, all at once a sound came from heaven like that of a strong wind blowing, and filled the whole house where they were sitting. Then appeared to them what seemed to be tongues of fire, which parted and came to rest on each of them; and they were all filled with the Holy Spirit, and began to speak in strange languages, as the Spirit gave utterance to each." (Acts 2.1–4.) The effect of the gift of the Spirit on the first community was immediate and striking. They were indeed filled with "power from on high". (Luke 24.49.) And the rest of the Book of Acts is a testimony to the presence and work of the Spirit in the primitive Church.

The gift of the Spirit was not confined to those who had been gathered together on the day of Pentecost. What had happened on that day was the realization of the prophecies that the Spirit would be poured out on all men. In his sermon immediately after the event Peter said: "This is what was foretold by the prophet Joel: In the last times, God says, I will pour out my spirit upon all mankind, and your sons and daughters will be prophets. Your young men shall see visions, and your old men shall dream dreams; and I will pour out my spirit in those days upon my servants and handmaids, so that they will prophesy." (Acts 2.16–18.) The gift of the Spirit was now available to all.

But how were others to receive it? When Peter had finished speaking, his listeners, moved by his words, asked, "Brethren, what must we do? Repent, Peter said to them, and be baptized, every one of you, in the name of Jesus Christ, to have your sins forgiven; then you will receive the gift of the Holy Spirit. This promise is for you and for your children, and for all those, however far away, whom the Lord our God calls to himself." (Acts 2.37–9.) Baptism is a first requirement; the gift of the Spirit followed upon it. This was the order of events unless God intervened in a special way. He did so in the case of Cornelius. We are told that after Peter had finished speaking to Cornelius and his household "the Holy Spirit fell on all those who were listening to his message". (Acts 10.44.) It was this that convinced Peter that these people, though Gentiles, should be baptized. "Then Peter said openly, Who will grudge us the water for baptizing these men, that have received the Holy Spirit just as we did? And he gave orders that they should be baptized in the name of the Lord Jesus Christ." (Acts 10.47–8.) Although God gave the Spirit here directly as he did at Pentecost, a difference remained that kept the experience of Pentecost unique. Cornelius and his household had still to be joined to the Church by the sacrament of baptism. Pentecost transformed the first community into the Church; all others must be made members of that Church by baptism.

There are two texts in the Acts of the Apostles that associate the gift of the Spirit with a rite subsequent to baptism: an imposition of hands. The first text concerns the ministry of Philip the Deacon in Samaria. Philip preached the Gospel there. When people found faith he baptized them. The account continues: "And now the apostles at Jerusalem, hearing that Samaria had received the word of God, sent Peter and John to visit them. So these two came down and prayed for them, that they might receive the Holy Spirit, who had not, as yet, come down on any of them: they had received nothing so far except baptism in the name of the Lord Jesus. Then the apostles began to lay their hands on them, so that the Holy Spirit was given them."

(Acts 8.14–17.) Philip, then, baptized but did not impose hands to give the Holy Spirit; for this the Apostles had to come. The narrative goes on to tell how Simon Magus tried to buy the power of the Apostles with money.

The second text relates how Paul at Ephesus met a group of disciples of John the Baptist who had received John's baptism only. He discovered this by learning that they knew nothing about the Holy Spirit. He instructed them on the relation between John and Jesus. "On hearing this," we read, "they received baptism in the name of the Lord Jesus; and when Paul laid his hands upon them, the Holy Spirit came down on them, and they spoke with tongues, and prophesied." (Acts 19.5–6.) So, the Holy Spirit was given by the laying on of hands.

In these texts of the Acts (including the sermon of Peter) a distinction is made between the effect of baptism and the effect of the imposition of hands. Baptism remits sin and is the entry into the Church; the imposition of hands gives the Spirit. This presentation would seem to mark an early, undeveloped stage in the theology of baptism. Certainly, the prominence John gives to water as a symbol of the Spirit implies that for him the Spirit was given in the waters of baptism. However, outside the Acts the two rites of initiation are not distinguished in the

New Testament, nor is there any demarcation of their effects. There is a text in Hebrews that mentions the laying on of hands among the elementary doctrines in which Christians were first instructed (Heb. 6.2), and this is usually taken as a reference to the second rite of initiation. Some have seen in Verse 4 of the same chapter an allusion to the three sacraments of Christian initiation, namely baptism, confirmation and the Eucharist. The verse runs: "We can do nothing for those who have received, once for all, their enlightenment, who have tasted the heavenly gift, partaken of the Holy Spirit, known, too, God's word of comfort, and the powers that belong to a future life, and then fallen away." (Heb. 6.4–5.) Their enlightenment was their baptism; they tasted the heavenly gift in the Eucharist, after having partaken of the Holy Spirit in confirmation. The text, however, is not sufficiently clear to provide us with an adequate basis for distinguishing the effects of baptism and the imposition of hands.

The relation between baptism and confirmation is still a difficult problem. It is a matter for theological discussion, and there are differing views even among Catholic theologians. There are two main reasons for the difficulty of the problem. The first is the fact that the two sacraments were so bound up together in the first

centuries that their effects were not distinguished
with precision. Christian initiation, consisting of
baptism, confirmation and the Eucharist, took
place all at once and formed a unity. The Eucharist stood out because it was not confined to
Christian initiation but celebrated repeatedly
by all Christians. But baptism and confirmation
remained merged into one. In the early centuries
the word "baptism" was used for the whole rite,
including both sacraments, as can be discerned
from various texts. The same is true of the word
sphragis (meaning "seal"), which plays an important part in the patristic teaching on the
effect of Christian initiation and on the gift of
the Spirit. The name "confirmation" (*confirma-
tio*) for the second rite of initiation first appears
in Gaul at the Council of Riez in 439 and the
Council of Orange in 441. The second reason
that makes the problem of the relation between
baptism and confirmation a difficult one is the
instability of the rite of confirmation. From the
point of view of ritual, confirmation has not
remained identical with itself. Christian initiation soon included several post-baptismal rites.
Which is to be taken as the essential rite of confirmation? It is not an easy question to answer,
and history shows that now one rite, now another, was regarded as the essential part. Consequently the external rite itself does not convey

an altogether clear message on the effects of the sacrament.

We must not, however, exaggerate the obscurity that remains. Much has been written on confirmation in recent years, and it is possible to present teaching of considerable richness on the sacrament. If the line between baptism and confirmation is still somewhat blurred, this need not worry us unduly. These sacraments do form a close unity and both are needed to make us fully Christians.

Two things must be done to get a better understanding of confirmation. First, we must examine the history of the post-baptismal rites and the place of confirmation among them. Then, in the light of this and helped by the teaching of tradition, we must try to determine the proper effect of confirmation in relation to baptism. This chapter will give the history of the rites, the next will discuss the effect of the second stage of Christian initiation.

As we have already seen, the texts of the New Testament bear witness to a second rite alongside the baptismal rite, namely an imposition of hands together with a prayer to the Holy Spirit, a rite that had an outpouring of the Spirit as its effect and which was therefore a means of grace complementary to baptism. Now, in the period immediately following the New Testament there is little evidence for any post-baptismal rite. It is only in the third century that we begin to get some definite information. But meanwhile a rite of anointing after baptism had been introduced in some regions.

The first testimonies to a post-baptismal anointing come from the second century. It is described as a rite customary among the gnostic sects by St. Irenaeus, and it is also mentioned in the *Excerpta*, a collection of texts from Theodotus, a disciple of the gnostic Valentinus, made by Clement of Alexandria. In both cases the gnostic usage seems to be one borrowed from the Catholic Church. We can conclude that the use of chrism in the Church goes back a while, possibly to the end of the first century. A passage in the second-century Latin writer Tertullian confirms this. He attacks the Marcionite heretics, who were akin to the gnostics, for their inconsistency in using material things in their initiation rites, while regarding matter as evil. (See *Adversus Marcionem*, 1, 14.) Marcion left the Church in July 144. It is unlikely that he or his disciples would have introduced the initiation rites, considering their aversion from material things. Anointing, then, must have been generally accepted before 144. At all events, we have testimonies to the anointing as a rite of the Church from the third century onwards.

The use of the word *sphragis* ("seal") for Christian initiation may have had something to do with the introduction of this anointing. The purpose would have been to express the interior effect of the imposition of hands by adding a new symbolic rite. There are passages in the New Testament which speak of Christians as being sealed by the Spirit and references also to a spiritual anointing. Thus: "In him [Christ] you too learned to believe, and had the seal set on your faith by the promised gift of the Holy Spirit" (Eph. 1.13); "Do not distress God's holy Spirit, whose seal you bear until the day of your redemption comes" (Eph. 4.30); "It is God who gives both us and you our certainty in Christ; it is he who has anointed us, just as it is he who has put his seal on us, and given us the foretaste of his Spirit in our hearts" (2 Cor. 1.21–2); "Meanwhile, the influence of his anointing lives on in you." (1 John 2.27.) In these texts it is not a question of a ritual signing or anointing. Although it is not difficult to see in them an allusion to the sacraments of Christian initiation, the expressions they use refer to the interior effects, not to the external rites. But it is not surprising that Christians should have been led to express the inward sealing, or signing, and spiritual anointing, in an external anointing done in an action of signing.

5

In using oil—which means olive oil, the oil *par excellence* in the Mediterranean countries—for her liturgy, the Church was continuing a practice of the Old Testament. The Hebrews poured out oil on holy stones and other objects and anointed kings, priests and prophets with it. The primitive origin of this custom is not clear. It has been suggested[1] that the original reason for using it was similar to the reason for the parallel use of blood. Blood was thought to be the seat of life, or even life itself. The fat of an animal was likewise considered as associated in a special way with its life. The oil of the olive may have been taken in a similar way as possessing the spirit of life, so that anointing with it would have been regarded as a means of giving life, or more life, to the person anointed. This primitive meaning was later lost sight of. At any rate, the meaning actually given to an anointing with sacred oil was the bestowal of holiness. The person or thing anointed was brought into contact with the divine; the anointed was sanctified by Yahweh, the Holy One. Anointing, too, was closely associated with the giving of the Spirit. What may have been a symbol of renewed strength and vitality became a symbol of contact with the holiness of God and of the giving of the

[1] See J. van der Ploeg, O.P., "Old Testament Signs", *Scripture*, 8 (1956), pp. 42-3.

Spirit. The Christian use is in line with this, and also exploits the fact that it was kings, priests and prophets who were anointed.

Etymologically, the word "chrism" simply means "oil for anointing" (cf. "Christ", meaning "Anointed"), but it is reserved for what was formerly called the oil of thanksgiving, as distinct from the oil of exorcism (or of catechumens) and the oil of the sick. It is the oil for the post-baptismal anointings, including confirmation. Chrism is marked out from the other two sacred oils by the admixture of balsam (in the East other perfumes are added as well) and by the solemnity of its consecration. This consecration was reserved to the bishop even in the early centuries when priests were allowed to bless the other oils. In the Western Church since about the sixth century the practice has been to bless all three oils on the morning of Maundy Thursday. There is a special mass for this purpose in each cathedral. The ceremony is a very impressive one, the bishop being assisted by twelve priests, seven deacons and seven subdeacons. The ritual goes back in its essentials to the eighth century, but the consecratory prayer for the chrism was used already in the sixth century. Like the prayer that consecrates the baptismal water, this prayer sung over the chrism is very rich in teaching. It is important for an understanding of the meaning the Church attaches to chrism and its uses, and the pity is that it remains completely unknown to most Catholics.

Anointing, then, as we have seen, was introduced at an early date as a post-baptismal rite. At first it existed alongside the imposition of hands. But in the East the anointing rapidly ousted the earlier rite altogether. The anointing now stood alone as the rite conferring the Holy Spirit. This is the situation we find revealed in the *Mystagogical Catecheses* written in the fourth century by St. Cyril of Jerusalem or his successor in the see, John. These *Mystagogical Catecheses* are instructions given to the neophytes during Easter Week, explaining to them the rites they have just undergone. Now, in his commentary on the initiation rites,[1] Cyril says nothing about any imposition of hands, but he describes the ceremony of anointing that followed baptism. The baptized were anointed on the forehead, the ears, the nose and the breast, and this anointing is stated to be the sign of the Holy Spirit. St. Cyril, however, was well aware that in apostolic times the Holy Spirit was given by an imposition of hands, because in the *Catechetical Lectures*, which were delivered to the candidates for baptism during Lent (and cer-

[1] For the relevant passages, see Whitaker, *Documents*, pp. 20–7.

tainly composed by Cyril), mention is made of this. He goes on to say that he will tell them later how they themselves will receive the Holy Spirit. If we take it that this promise was fulfilled in the later instruction after baptism, then we can conclude that Cyril saw the anointing as replacing the earlier imposition of hands as the rite conferring the Holy Spirit.

At all events, most of the present Eastern liturgies preserve no trace of an imposition of hands. The rite of confirmation is limited to an anointing of the forehead and other parts of the body. Thus in the Byzantine rite the sacrament is given in this way. It is given immediately after baptism, and the anointing ceremony begins with thanksgiving for the baptismal grace and prayer for the coming gift of the Spirit. The priest then anoints the child with the sign of the cross on the forehead, eyes, nostrils, lips, ears, breast, hands and feet, saying each time, "The seal of the gift of the Holy Spirit, Amen."

Although the imposition of hands was generally abandoned in the East, it was kept in the Coptic and Ethiopian rites, which have it still. These are rites belonging to the patriarchate of Alexandria, which came under the influence of Rome through the translations of the *Apostolic Tradition* of Hippolytus.

Before I turn to the history of confirmation in the West, I must mention the puzzling practice of the early Syrian Church, which creates a problem not yet adequately solved by theologians. It warns us not to be too rigid in determining and explaining the Church's sacramental ritual. The practice of the Church has been surprisingly flexible.

The *Didascalia Apostolorum* is a Syrian Church Order of the third century, giving us the practice of the West Syrians. In its account of baptism, there is first an anointing of the head done by the bishop with an imposition of hands, then an anointing of the whole body carried out by one of the ministers or by the deaconesses for women, and this is followed by the baptism itself. The author alludes elsewhere to an imposition of hands during the baptism, but it is not clear whether this is distinct from the preceding imposition. At any rate, there is no mention of any anointing after the baptism. Likewise in the fourth century, John Chrysostom, in his catechetical instructions at Antioch, mentions only two rites: the prebaptismal anointing and the baptism with water. His compatriot and contemporary, Theodore of Mopsuestia, in his catechetical instructions, mentions the prebaptismal anointing, the baptism with water, during which there was an imposition of hands, and then afterwards a signing on the forehead of the baptized. There is no indication that this signing is done with oil.

What are we to make of this evidence? Was there a rite of confirmation distinct from that of baptism? Some, basing themselves on the allusion in the *Didascalia*, have thought that confirmation was given by an imposition of hands. But others have suggested that at this early period in Syria baptism and confirmation were conferred simultaneously by the same rites. Towards the end of the fourth century, the *Apostolic Constitutions*, a Church Order from the same region, attests the existence of a post-baptismal anointing.

In East Syria, the *Liturgical Homilies* of Narsai of Nisibis give us the practice of the fifth century. Again, there is no mention of a post-baptismal anointing or laying on of hands. The later liturgical documents do, however, clearly indicate confirmation. Sometimes it is given by the imposition of hands alone, sometimes with an anointing as well. Perhaps we can conclude from this that the anointing was added later to a previously existing imposition of hands. But the evidence is not clear.

To turn now to the West. We must first consider briefly the liturgies outside Rome. It must be remembered that it was not until a later date that the West as a whole adopted the Roman rite.

Unlike the Roman liturgy, which from the time of Hippolytus had two distinct post-baptismal anointings, the other Western liturgies had only one such anointing, which came immediately after the baptism with water. In Africa and Spain, it was followed simply by the laying on of hands. In Milan and Gaul, the anointing was followed by two rites: the washing of feet and the laying on of hands.

Tertullian, an African writer, is the only one who mentions a signing among the post-baptismal rites. Even so, he does not do so in his work on baptism, *De Baptismo*, but in a passage of *De Resurrectione Carnis* (ch. 8), which does however seem to list the rites of initiation:

> Flesh is washed, that the soul may be cleansed:
> flesh is anointed, that the soul may be consecrated:
> flesh is signed, that the soul may be fortified:
> flesh is shadowed by the imposition of the hand, that the soul may be enlightened by the Spirit:
> flesh feeds on the body and blood of Christ, that the soul also may fatten upon God.[1]

[1] Whitaker, p. 9.

St. Cyprian, another African writer, a little later than Tertullian, is often quoted as bearing witness to a rite of signing after baptism, but this interpretation is denied.[1] Cyprian speaks indeed of signing and uses the expression "the seal of the Lord" (*signaculum dominicum*), but like St. Paul he is referring not to an external rite but to the interior effects produced by the Spirit.

Two rites, then, are chiefly in question, an anointing and an imposition of hands. Now, the Council of Orange in 441 makes it clear in its second canon[2] that the anointing belongs to baptism and not to confirmation. We can take it, then, that in these Western liturgies the post-baptismal anointing was understood as forming one with the rite of immersion and completing it symbolically. The negative effect of baptism, the cleansing from sin, was associated with the immersion, while the positive effects constituting holiness were attached to the anointing. This is still the view reflected in the prayer for the consecration of the chrism. In contrast with water

[1] See R. Béraudy in *L'Église en prière: Introduction à la liturgie*, ed. A. G. Martimort, Paris and Tournai (1961), p. 554. I wish here to acknowledge my debt to this book, on which I have drawn largely for this history of confirmation and for the previous chapter on the baptismal rite.

[2] Whitaker, p. 216.

understood as bringing remission of sins, the oil is presented as the cause of life, holiness and peace. The anointing makes one sacrament with the immersion. The rite of confirmation was the imposition of hands that followed. Unlike the East, the West retained this as the essential rite for the second stage of Christian initiation. It was accompanied by a prayer asking for the gift of the Spirit to be given to those who were now baptized. This prayer was called a *benedictio* or *invocatio*; very soon it included a list of the seven gifts of the Holy Spirit, as was the custom in Rome.

Such, then, was the rite of confirmation in the West outside Rome: an imposition of hands with a prayer. The rite of the Church of Milan as reflected in the writings of St. Ambrose in the fourth century might at first sight seem to have been different. St. Ambrose speaks of the *invocatio*, but does not mention the gesture that accompanied it. At the same time, he talks of a signing and uses the expression "spiritual seal" (*signaculum spiritale*). But it is unlikely that at Milan the *invocatio* was not accompanied by an imposition of hands, as it was everywhere else in the West. As for his remarks about a spiritual seal, these are to be interpreted, as with St. Cyprian, of the interior effects, not of an external rite.

The development of confirmation in the Roman rite is more complicated. Eventually this development concerned the whole Western Church, and modifications to the rite came from outside Rome. The history of it opens with the *Apostolic Tradition* of Hippolytus, a work that takes us back to the beginning of the third century. Already at that time in Rome there were two post-baptismal anointings, one forming a part of baptism and the other attached to confirmation. But there was also an imposition of hands, and so the subsequent history of confirmation largely concerns the relation of the anointing and this imposition of hands.

Here is the rite as described by Hippolytus. After the immersion, the baptized are anointed with the oil of thanksgiving by the priest. They dry themselves, put on their clothes and go to the place of assembly, the church. There the bishop lays his hand upon them, with a prayer that asks God to send the Holy Spirit upon them. It is not clear whether this imposition of hands is done over all of them together, or is an individual imposition on each candidate. A collective imposition seems more probable in view of the fact that the prayer accompanying it is given in the plural. After the imposition the bishop pours consecrated oil over each candidate, and laying his hand on the head, says: "I anoint

thee with the holy oil in God the Father Almighty and Christ Jesus and the Holy Ghost."
Then he seals, that is, signs, him on the forehead
and gives him the kiss of peace. Thus, we have
an imposition of hands with a prayer, an anointing with a second imposition of hands and an
indicative formula, and a signing on the forehead but without oil.

We are fairly well informed from various
documents about the rite of confirmation at
Rome in the period from the fifth to the eighth
centuries. It remained much the same as in the
time of Hippolytus. But some changes may be
noted. The first, apparently collective, imposition of hands remained, but the prayer accompanying it developed. We know from a remark
of Pope Siricius that already in the fourth century it included a mention of the seven gifts of
the Holy Spirit. The actual prayer which the
bishop says at the beginning of our present rite
when he extends his hands over all the candidates together is found in the sixth century in
the *Gelasian Sacramentary*, except that the
Amens now said after the mention of each gift
of the Spirit are not given and the formula of
conclusion immediately follows the mention of
the seventh gift. The clause that now follows that
mention, "... and in thy goodness mark them
out for eternal life with the sign of the cross of

Christ" ("et consigna eos signo crucis Christi in vitam propitiatus aeternam"), was added a little later. Another change that took place was the combining of the anointing and the signing. The person was now anointed by a signing on the forehead, with a consequent dropping of the second imposition of hands. The combination came about fairly early; for a letter of Pope Innocent I bears witness to it in the fifth century. In the *Gelasian Sacramentary* this signing with chrism is accompanied by the formula, "The sign of Christ unto eternal life" ("Signum Christi in vitam aeternam"), but another formula in widespread use was the simple "In the name of the Father and of the Son and of the Holy Ghost" ("In nomine Patris et Filii et Spiritus Sancti"). Our present formula, "I sign thee with the sign of the cross and I confirm thee with the chrism of salvation", is first found in the book known as the Roman Pontifical of the twelfth century.

This latter document introduced an individual laying on of hands at the beginning of the confirmation rite. It comes before the ancient invocation of the Holy Spirit and is accompanied by the short prayer, "May the Holy Ghost come down upon you, and may the power of the Most High God keep you free from every sin." This prayer still comes at the beginning of our present rite, though without the imposition of hands that went with it in the twelfth century. In the Pontifical of Durandus of the thirteenth century, the individual imposition is already omitted, and instead there is again a collective imposition, but now by an extension of both hands over the candidates during the ancient invocation of the Holy Spirit. This corresponds to our present rubrics.

The rite of confirmation given in the Pontifical of Durandus is in fact the same as we have today apart from two small variations. The formula he has for the anointing is slightly longer by the inclusion of a further clause. Further, the bishop anoints the forehead without laying his hand on the head, since this practice was introduced only in the eighteenth century.

The prayers that follow the anointing in Durandus and in our present rite owe their origin to the separation of confirmation from baptism. The separation of the two sacraments began in the rural parishes already in the fourth and fifth centuries because the bishop could not be present at the baptisms in all the parishes. Nevertheless, for a long time the two sacraments were given together whenever a bishop was present. It was not until much later that confirmation was deferred as a general rule. At all events, it was the isolation of confirmation that created the need for additions to its rite. It was provided with various opening and closing ceremonies. What we have at the end of our present rite is a verse from the Bible sung as an antiphon (*Confirma hoc*), some versicles and responses, the prayer *Deus qui apostolis tuis*, and some more biblical verses used somewhat unusually as a formula for the final blessing. The most important of the additions is the prayer *Deus qui apostolis tuis*. It goes back to the ninth century and came into the Roman liturgy in the tenth. We can draw a twofold teaching from it: the Spirit in confirmation is the Spirit given to the Apostles at Pentecost, and the coming of the Spirit completes the work of baptism by making the confirmed living temples of his glory. This prayer originally preceded the final verses that are now used us a blessing. The positions were reversed in the Pontifical of Durandus.

By Durandus, then, in the thirteenth century, the development of the Roman rite of confirmation was completed to all intents and purposes. The rite almost exactly as he gave it was taken over by the official Roman Pontifical of 1485. But how are we to understand the rite? We have a collective imposition of hands with a solemn invocation of the Holy Spirit and then an anointing done with a signing and accompanied by an indicative formula. The signing was originally distinct from the anointing. They were joined up in the fifth century or before. Since the eighteenth century, an imposition of hands has been added to the signing. Which is the essential rite in this complex of rites? The answer given has varied in the course of centuries.

Right up to the time of Gregory the Great in the sixth century, the imposition of hands with the invocation of the Spirit was taken to be the sole essential rite of confirmation. This was the rite that conferred the seal of the Spirit. It was probably because the imposition was done over all together that a signing of the forehead was added to indicate the application to each candidate of the effect produced by the general imposition of hands.

However, in the fifth century, Pope Innocent I reserved not only the imposition of hands but also the anointing of the forehead to the bishop. This prescription caused the two rites to be regarded as on an equal footing, so that now it was thought that the bishop confirmed by both rites together. This point of view is expressly stated by Pope Gregory II in the eighth century.

From the ninth century onwards the liturgical books stress so much the combined rite of signing and anointing that it seems to be regarded as the sole essential rite. The theologians at first did not like to admit the absence of an imposition of hands in confirmation, because this was the rite given in Scripture. But they no longer pay any attention to the extension of hands at the beginning of the rite. Instead, some find an imposition of hands in the anointing itself, since the bishop does touch the candidate in signing his forehead. This teaching is reflected in the Second Council of Lyons of 1274, which stated: "The sacrament of confirmation, which bishops confer by the imposition of hands in anointing those who have been reborn." (Denzinger, 465.) The great scholastic writers, however, felt no scruple about the loss of the imposition of hands. They declare without hesitation that the essential matter of confirmation is the anointing, the essential form the words that accompany it. This rite is seen as replacing the apostolic rite of the imposition of hands recorded in Scripture. This teaching was taken over by the Church. The Council of Florence in the fifteenth century repeats St. Thomas's teaching, and presents the anointing as replacing the primitive imposition of hands. The Council of Trent speaks of the chrismation but makes no mention of any imposition of hands.

In the eighteenth century Pope Benedict XIV, a scholar-pope, wishing to re-establish a continuity with ancient practice, introduced an imposition of hands into the rite of anointing. The bishop was instructed to lay his hand flat on the candidate's head while he signed the forehead with his thumb moist with oil. That is still the present usage. This imposition of the hand is not, however, necessary for validity.

So, as I said, from the standpoint of its ritual, confirmation has not remained identical with itself. The original essential rite in the Roman liturgy was the general imposition of hands with the invocation of the Holy Spirit. This still remains, but it is now an accessory rite. According to replies given by the Holy See, the sacrament is not repeated, even conditionally, if this rite has been omitted. An anointing was introduced at a very early date into the confirmation ritual. It is now the essential rite in the West as well as in the East.

We can now take a brief, comprehensive look at our present rite of confirmation.

It is customary to open the ceremony with the hymn *Veni Creator Spiritus*, followed by a talk from the bishop. The bishop then stands facing the candidates and says the first short prayer asking for the Holy Spirit to come down upon them. This is followed by several versicles and responses, and then the bishop stretches out his hands over the candidates, indicating in this dramatic gesture that he is going to hand on to them the Holy Spirit, and at the same time utters the ancient, solemn invocation of the Spirit and his gifts. It is interspersed with Amens.

The candidates afterwards go up in turn for the anointing, which is given in the way just described. The gesture is now a threefold sign. First, the laying on of the bishop's hand, which is a basic, human gesture of commissioning, a giving of power and authority to perform some task. It indicates that by confirmation we are appointed to the status of witnesses to Christ. Second, the consecration with chrism. Chrism is olive oil mixed with balsam. It is a sign that we are penetrated with the Spirit and made like to Christ, the Anointed. Its sweet smell reminds us that we must spread the knowledge of God abroad everywhere, like a perfume. Third, the tracing of the sign of the cross. We are marked with the sign of Christ on our foreheads because we must profess our faith openly without shame. The cross is the sign of suffering; we must be prepared to suffer for Christ with the strength given by the Holy Spirit. The cross is the sign of victory: Christ saved the world through the cross. The cross is the sign of glory: sealed with the sign of Christ we are marked out for glory.

The bishop strikes each candidate lightly on the cheek when he has anointed him. The touch is a caress, a short form of the ancient kiss of peace. It is a sign of love and affection from the bishop as he welcomes us as new workers in the field of Christ. Durandus in the thirteenth century was the first to interpret this gesture as a slap, giving it the mistaken symbolism of the blows and sufferings we must undergo in the service of Christ.

After the individual anointings there are the prayers for the confirmed, particularly the *Deus qui apostolis tuis*. The bishop then gives a concluding blessing with a special formula. Usually, everyone then joins in saying the Apostles' Creed, the Our Father and the Hail Mary; and Benediction is given.

The ordinary minister of confirmation is the bishop. It has remained the normal rule in the Western Church that confirmation should be given personally by the bishop. This has led to the separation of the two sacraments of baptism and confirmation, which were formerly given together. The problem of the impossibility of the bishop's presence at all baptisms was solved differently in the East. Priests were authorized to give confirmation. This custom is found already in the fourth century, as we know from the work entitled *The Apostolic Constitutions* from that century. Although it is now the priest who generally confirms in the East, the sacrament keeps a relation to the bishop inasmuch as he alone consecrates the chrism. In 1946 the Pope gave parish priests the power to confirm their subjects when in danger of death. When a priest thus receives the authority to confirm, it does not mean that he is raised by papal decree, as it were, to the episcopal state. He remains simply a priest. The point is that the Church has the power, within limits, to vary the minister of a sacrament, just as she has the power, within limits, to vary the sacramental rite itself. Whether bishop or priest is the designated minister, the power of the sacrament comes from Christ who uses either as his minister.

What the history of the confirmation rite shows us is that the sacraments are the activity of Christ's Church. They are not inanimate things like charms; they are not magical rites to be repeated without understanding; they are the activity of the Church as a community. Hence they are marked by her history. The vicissitudes of her life are reflected in the history of her sacraments. While she must keep within the limits of Christ's institution, those limits are evidently wide enough to allow a considerable measure of adaptation to changing outlooks and conditions.

WITNESSES OF CHRIST

HOWEVER difficult it may be to determine the precise effect of confirmation in relation to baptism, there is one statement clear throughout tradition that may serve as a starting-point for reflection on the sacrament: confirmation is the completion, the finishing or perfecting of baptism. The second sacrament is there to complete the work of initiation begun by the first sacrament, baptism.

It is true we must not forget that there is yet a third sacrament of initiation: the Holy Eucharist. In the early Church the neophytes went immediately after their baptism and confirmation into the assembly of the faithful to take part in the offering of the Eucharist and receive communion. Their entry was an impressive affair in some places. They came in procession, holding lighted candles and singing Psalm 22, "The Lord is my shepherd". Another practice is also of interest. Hippolytus tells us that in Rome at their first communion neophytes were given a mixture of milk and honey as well as the bread and wine. This custom was still in use in the sixth century, when John the Deacon mentions it in a letter that has survived. He says that the milk and honey represent the Promised Land, which is the land of the Resurrection, the inheritance of the baptized. The Eucharist, then, was undoubtedly seen as completing Christian initiation. This was a true insight. The Eucharist contains the mystery of Christ's death and resurrection, and by celebrating it we enter more fully into the mystery we began to share at baptism. When we receive the body and blood of Christ our incorporation into him is perfected: "We have a cup that we bless; is not this cup we bless a participation in Christ's blood? Is not the bread we break a participation in Christ's body? The one bread makes us one body, though we are many in number; the same bread is shared by all." (1 Cor. 10.16–17.) The Eucharist therefore completes what baptism begins. It alone brings the fullness of the Christian life, and we can say that the purpose of baptism and confirmation is to prepare us for the Eucharist. They are our entry into the banquet of the Eucharist, where our union with Christ and through Christ with the Father is fully accomplished.

All the same, the celebration of the Eucharist is constantly repeated, whereas baptism and confirmation are received once for all. Hence, confirmation does in a certain sense complete the initiation of a Christian. It brings a perfective grace that establishes a person fully within the Church, with all the responsibilities and privileges of a full Christian, able to take part fully in all the activities proper to Christians, chief among which is the Eucharist. Confirmation makes us complete Christians, fully established in the Christian state, with our definitive, unrepeatable initiation finished. That is what is meant by the familiar phrase of the Catechism which tells us that confirmation makes us "perfect Christians"; but the word "perfect" is misleading, since the correct meaning is "full" or "complete", not "advanced in the spiritual life". We know that at the time of our confirmation we are very far from being "perfect Christians" in the ordinary understanding of the phrase. We do, however, become full Christians in the sense of reaching our full status within the Church.

Confirmation is now usually separated from baptism by a considerable interval, but the link between the two is still declared in the invocation of the Holy Spirit said by the bishop as he stretches out his hands over the candidates: "Almighty, everlasting God, who hast given new life through water and the Holy Ghost to these thy servants and granted them forgiveness of all their sins, send down upon them from heaven thy Holy Spirit the Paraclete with his sevenfold gifts." The prayer presents confirmation as following upon baptismal regeneration through water and the Holy Spirit and completing it by the further gift of the Spirit.

Under the truth that confirmation makes us complete Christians we can put the familiar teaching of St. Thomas that this sacrament makes us adults in the Christian life. He draws a comparison between bodily life and the life of grace and sees confirmation as the sacrament of maturity. He writes: "Coming of age ends a definite period; after that a man is capable of acting for himself: 'When I was a child, I spoke as a child, I understood as a child, I thought as a child; but when I became a man, I put away childish things.' (1 Cor. 13.11.) By the process of being born we receive bodily life: by the process of growing up we become adult. So is it in the life of the spirit; born by baptism, we reach our full stature by confirmation."[1] So, by baptism we were born to a new life. We became sons of God and members of the Church. But before confirmation we were but young children in the Christian life. Confirmation makes us Christian adults, with the fullness of the Spirit and, as I shall explain later, a responsible part in the work

[1] *Summa Theologica*, III, qu. 72, a. 1. Translation from Thomas Gilby, *St. Thomas Aquinas: Theological Texts*, Oxford (1955), no. 608.

of the Church. Confirmation is thus the sacrament of Christian manhood. The Eucharist is
the sacrament of Christian growth in the sense
of providing the means for continuous progress
in the Christian life. But confirmation is the
sacrament of maturity inasmuch as it marks the
transition from childhood to adulthood, which
occurs only once. Without confirmation a baptized person is an incomplete Christian in the
same way as a child is not yet completely a man.

What has been said so far confronts us with a
problem, which must be examined before
further analysing the perfective grace of confirmation. When should confirmation be given?
Without confirmation a person is an incomplete
Christian; with confirmation a person is an adult
Christian. Of these two statements, the first
seems to urge confirmation at an early age, the
second suggests that a later age would be more
suitable. Which alternative is right?

Originally, baptism, confirmation and the
Eucharist, the three sacraments of initiation,
were given in that order at one celebration to
both infants and adults. This practice manifested the unity of Christian initiation most
clearly. But the growth of the Church and its
extension from town to country created a difficult problem. It became impossible for the
bishop to be present at all baptisms. As I said in

the last chapter, East and West solved the problem in different ways. In the East the primitive unity of the three sacraments was kept by allowing priests to administer confirmation. This is still the Eastern practice, and moreover communion is still given to infants after their baptism and confirmation. In the West, confirmation remained reserved to the bishop. He is the head of the Christian community and should, it was felt, be the one to complete the acceptance of a person into that community. The insistence upon this led to an increasing separation of confirmation and baptism from the fourth century onwards. Nevertheless, up to the twelfth century, the three sacraments were given together whenever a bishop was available, and no distinction was made in the manner of conferring Christian initiation on adults and infants. When possible, even infants were given baptism, confirmation and communion in immediate succession; where confirmation was delayed, the sacraments were still received in that order.

From the end of the twelfth century the practice spread of not giving communion to infants or children before what was called the age of discretion. Since it had been found difficult to give communion under both kinds to newly-born infants, the custom had grown up after the tenth century of giving them just a few drops of the wine. This practice was dropped when the faithful no longer communicated under both kinds, which was by about the beginning of the thirteenth century. The Fourth Lateran Council in 1215, by laying down the obligation of an annual Easter communion only for those who had reached the age of discretion, implicitly approved the practice of delaying communion until that age. It was already the general custom by then, and it has remained so ever since. However, there have been various interpretations of the age of discretion. At various times and places we find the age of discretion taken as somewhere between seven and twelve or frequently even as fourteen or fifteen.

Shortly after the Lateran Council the custom began of deferring confirmation. The practice was not uniform; it was deferred until the age of one or three or seven or even twelve. Nevertheless, it was always given before communion. The Catechism of the Council of Trent, issued in 1566, had the effect of firmly establishing the practice of not giving confirmation before the age of seven, referred to as the age of reason. It stated: "Here it is to be observed, that, after Baptism, the Sacrament of Confirmation may indeed be administered to all; but that, until children shall have attained the use of reason, its administration is inexpedient. If it does not seem well to defer [Confirmation] to the age of twelve, it is most proper to postpone this Sacrament at least to that of seven years."[1] Not before seven but not later than twelve became the general practice in the West, except in some dioceses of Spain and Latin America where they still keep the custom of confirming infants in connection with baptism. All the same, it remained the practice everywhere for centuries to give confirmation before communion. It was not until after the French Revolution, and then especially from about the middle of the nineteenth century, that the custom grew up of leaving confirmation until after first communion. It arose in France, spread first to Belgium and then to Austro-Hungary. The decree *Quam Singulari* of 1910, which brought first communion back to the age of seven, gave this reversal of order between confirmation and communion a firm hold. It has become so much the accepted usage that some people have the idea that it is wrong for a child to be confirmed before its first communion, even when this is feasible.

A reaction has developed in recent decades in favour of a return to the old order of baptism,

[1] *Catechism of the Council of Trent for Parish Priests*, translated into English with notes by John A. McHugh, O.P. and Charles J. Callan, O.P., New York (1936), p. 208.

confirmation and communion, or at least to confirmation at an early age. This movement can claim some support from various Roman decisions.

In 1917 the Code of Canon Law made this law about the age of confirmation: ". . . although the administration of the sacrament of confirmation in the Latin Church is fittingly deferred until about the seventh year of age, it may be given earlier if a child is in danger of death or if the minister considers it expedient for just and serious reasons." (Canon 788.) In 1931 the Commission for the Interpretation of the Code was asked whether this law meant that confirmation must not be given in the Latin Church before about the seventh year, except in the instances mentioned. The reply affirmed that this was the correct interpretation. Other documents from Rome indicate the need for some instruction prior to confirmation.

At the same time, Rome seems to consider it desirable and normal that children should receive confirmation before first communion. A reply of the Sacred Congregation of the Sacraments in 1932 dealt with the Spanish custom, already mentioned, of giving confirmation to infants. In the course of the reply the Sacred Congregation made this general observation: "Certainly it is opportune and more in conformity with the nature and effects of the sacrament of confirmation that children should not come to the Holy Table for the first time until they have received confirmation, which is like the complement of baptism and in which the Holy Spirit is given. . . . However, children must not be forbidden access to the Holy Table if they have come to the age of reason without having been able previously to receive the sacrament of confirmation." In other words, the primitive order is desirable, but the practical impossibility of getting confirmed must not delay first communion.

Other decrees from Rome bearing on this matter could be quoted, but it must be admitted that the support of Rome for the desire of an early confirmation about seven and before holy communion has been discreet so far. Those in favour of a later age find an argument for this from Rome's insistence on instruction before confirmation.

It is in France and Belgium that the movement towards an early confirmation before first communion has gained most ground. Liturgical and catechetical writings in the French language emphasize the fact that confirmation completes baptism and prepares the person for the Eucharist. It is argued that the deferment of the sacrament to the onset of adolescence involves a misunderstanding of its meaning. "There is no sacrament of adolescence", has been acidly remarked more than once. Confirmation is part of Christian initiation. It completes baptismal grace and is the proper preparation for communion. It gives the person his full rights as a member of the Church, with the function of bearing witness to the Faith. Once children have reached the age of reason and must profess their faith they should not be deprived of its grace. Confirmation is not ordered by its purpose as a sacrament to the personal spiritual struggle of adolescence: the sacraments for this are the Eucharist and penance.

This point of view has been officially sanctioned by the French hierarchy. Here are some extracts from the *Directory for the Sacraments* adopted by the French episcopate in 1951:

(31) The Church desires that confirmation be given at about the age of reason (the age, that is, of the so-called "private communion"). Should anyone say that "confirmation is the sacrament of adulthood", the answer is that the phrase must be understood of the spiritual and supernatural life, not of physical and social life on the natural level.

(32) ... it would be contrary to the intention of the Church to delay confirmation. The

faculties granted to parish priests to confer confirmation on the sick, even infants, clearly show this.

(33) Historically, confirmation is the second step in Christian initiation, and it is still linked with baptism in the Eastern Churches. Besides, confirmation gives, through the character, the necessary strength to those who receive it to bear authentic witness by professing the Faith both in acts of worship and in their lives. Confirmation, then, ought to be received before the Eucharist, especially in our times when children themselves are called upon to bear witness before a dechristianized world.[1]

This is clear enough. And the remark about understanding adulthood here in a spiritual sense can claim the express support of St. Thomas, who makes the same observation.[2]

German writers, however, take a different line, This can be seen by consulting Fr. Jungmann's important work, *Handing on the Faith: A Manual of Catechetics*.[3] Fr. Jungmann argues that the notion of confirmation as the comple-

[1] See *Directoire pour la pastorale des sacrements à l'usage du clergé*, Paris, Bonne Presse.

[2] *Summa Theologica*, III, q. 72, a. 8, ad. 2.

[3] Herder, Freiburg: London, Burns Oates (1959), pp. 340–46.

tion of baptism provides no indication of when this completion should be given. It is desirable that there should be an interval after first communion for further catechetical teaching. He suggests that the sacrament should come when childhood and religious instruction are at an end and the child goes out to confront the world for the first time. This is an important transition, needing to be marked by a sacrament; confirmation fits in well with it. Now, by our reckoning this would make confirmation very late indeed. I do not know enough about the school system in German-speaking countries to say which precise age Fr. Jungmann has in mind. At all events, it is clear that he wants confirmation not at seven but deferred to a later age to mark the end of childhood, understood not just in the spiritual sense but in the physical and intellectual sense.

A similar view is put forward by Fr. Fransen, writing in the new edition of the *Lexikon für Theologie und Kirche* and later in the Innsbruck *Zeitschrift*.[1]

In the *Lexikon* he recognizes that there has been some cautious Roman support for confirmation at an early age and also notes the

---

[1] Vol. 4, Freiburg (1960), s.v. "Firmung", pp. 151–2; "Erwägungen über das Firmalter", *Zeitschrift für katholische Theologie*, 84 (1962), pp. 401–26.

declaration of the French episcopate. But he goes on to say that the question is not a dogmatic one; it is one belonging to what may be called the Church's sacramental economy, the sphere of changing practice and adaptation to differing conditions. He then points out the desirability of some consecration to the apostolate and a sanctification of the transition to maturity and adult life. His conclusion is that, until Rome has made the matter more precise, the age of confirmation is a problem of pastoral practice coming within the competence of the bishop.

The later essay defends the same view, but with a depth of thought that makes it a valuable contribution to general sacramental theology. He distinguishes between the substance and essence of a sacrament. The substance is the sacramental reality as given by Christ himself; it is present in the sources of the Faith and preached by the Church, and embodied in a basic symbol to the extent that Christ himself has determined the sacramental sign or at least part of it. The essence is the concrete historical shape given to the sacrament by the Church, both in her teaching over the content of the sacrament and in the liturgical requirements for a valid administration. He then develops the distinction. Its relevance is that the essence of a sacrament is the sphere of the Church's economy in regard to the sacraments, that is, the range of her power to modify and adapt the sacraments to changing times and situations. Further, the fullness of sacramental mystery, the substance, is never exhaustively presented in the teaching and liturgy of the Church. Doctrinal teaching and liturgical symbolism can be more or less adequate, more or less complete as expressions of the sacramental mystery. The Church's management of the sacraments is not limited to ceremonial but achieves the adaptation of the sacraments at a deeper level.

It is in the light of these considerations—to which the few lines just given do scant justice —that Fr. Fransen tackles the question of the age of confirmation. He examines the theology and history of confirmation and finds no reason why a uniform solution should be imposed upon the whole Church. He admits that the traditional order of initiation, namely baptism, confirmation and the Eucharist, is a meaningful ideal of permanent value. But it is not the only factor that has to be considered. In these matters a choice must often be made. Important pastoral reasons of various kinds can demand that the Church, exercising her sacramental economy, leave aside this order the better to meet some situation. Other reasons against a late age for confirmation are likewise not of universal validity. Fr. Fransen does not put forward a late age as an ideal for the whole Church. What he urges is that the age of confirmation should be left for the local bishops to decide according to the pastoral necessities of their areas. He says that it would be regrettable if a single solution were imposed on the whole Church, seeing that the Church as a world Church faces varying and complex pastoral problems and has the power to adapt the sacraments to meet these.

Some writers in this country have urged a later age for confirmation. In 1955 Bishop Beck suggested that the sacrament should be linked to the transition from primary school to secondary school. He wrote: "The transition from primary to secondary school marks a real stage in a child's growing up. If the initiation to secondary school were accompanied by the reception of Confirmation, and the first year in the secondary school devoted to this theme, a profound effect might be produced in the minds of the boys and girls thus entering into a privileged group and acquiring special status in the Church."[1] The suggestion was taken up favourably by Canon Drinkwater in the catechetical journal *The Sower*, and in fact it corresponded to what he himself had previously advocated in

[1] "The School and the Parish", *The Clergy Review*, 40 (1955), p. 584.

regard to confirmation. Fr. Tynan, however, a well-known Irish educationalist, expressed serious doubts about such a plan, pointing out reasons for an early confirmation.[1] The impression I have received from talking to both priests and teachers is that the principle of confirmation at the age of eleven or twelve would meet with wide support in this country.

Thus, there are two views on the age of confirmation. I do not think that the theology of the sacrament provides a decisive answer to the question. Admittedly, some of the statements suggesting a late age for this sacrament do reflect an inadequate understanding of its meaning. It has been put forward as the sacrament of adolescence, the sacrament of Catholic Action, the sacrament that completes the period of religious formation: all these presentations unduly limit the scope of the sacrament. When one recalls the teaching of tradition on this sacrament as the completion of baptism, the sacrament of the Holy Spirit and the sacrament that prepares Christians for the Eucharist, it is easy to understand the reaction of the French theologians against the modern narrowing of the sacrament's purpose. But within the context of a true understanding of the sacrament, pastoral reasons

[1] "Confirmation at Eleven-Plus? A View from Ireland", *The Clergy Review*, 41 (1956), pp. 201–06.

may suggest a late age for its more effectual administration. The main argument, it seems to me, in favour of a later age is the desirability of a full personal participation in this sacrament, which is given only once. The necessity of baptism for salvation precludes a personal participation in their baptism by those born of Christian parents; they are baptized as infants. Is there not some advantage, particularly in the circumstances of a post-Christian society, in having a full, active, personal sharing in the second stage of initiation, confirmation? Presumably this is the reason for delaying confirmation until seven, the age of reason. But is not seven too early to secure an active, personal commitment to Christ in the full meaning of the phrase? It is objected to this that to delay confirmation is to upset the traditional order of the sacraments of initiation and take away part of the meaning of confirmation by making it follow first communion. But here facts must be faced, and we must talk about the real situation. Without wrongly deferring first communion, it is inevitable that most children will receive confirmation after their first communion. The ancient order will not in fact be observed, and arguments based upon it lose their force. That is, unless one is prepared to go as far as Dom B. Luykx and urge that parish priests should be given a general power to confirm, so that confirmation can be brought closely within the orbit of the parochial community.[1] Fr. Fransen deplores such a solution, and many will agree with him. Confirmation is the one solemn meeting between the individual Christian and his bishop: should we deprive him of it? Finally, Fr. Fransen's contention that a uniform solution should not be imposed on the whole Church is difficult to resist, either theologically or pastorally.

The statement that confirmation completes baptism and in that sense is the sacrament of Christian maturity led us into the long digression on the age of confirmation. But now I must pick up the earlier theme again and ask in what precise way confirmation completes baptism. This will show us what lies behind the discussions on the age of confirmation.

If it is clearly stated in tradition that confirmation completes baptism, it is equally clearly stated that this sacrament is the sacrament of the Holy Spirit.

This truth is clear from the rite itself. There is the ancient invocation of the Holy Spirit, which mentions each of the seven gifts. After

[1] In *La Confirmation: Doctrine et pastorale*, by Dom B. Luykx and Dom D. Scheyen, Bruges (1958), pp. 50–51. (Paroisse et liturgie: Collection de pastorale liturgique, no. 33.)

the anointing there is the prayer *Deus qui apostolis tuis* with its reference to Pentecost and to the coming of the Holy Spirit into the hearts of those just confirmed. The mention of Pentecost reminds us that in the New Testament the purpose of the rite of the laying on of hands was to give the Holy Spirit to those already baptized. Certainly, the connection of confirmation with the Holy Spirit is undeniable.

But this confronts us with the difficulty that most people feel about confirmation. Does not baptism itself make the person the dwelling-place of the Holy Spirit? Are not all the baptized, even before confirmation, temples of the Holy Spirit? How can confirmation bring the gift of the Holy Spirit?

In recent years a controversy on this point has taken place in the Church of England. The late Dom Gregory Dix published in 1946 a lecture entitled *The Theology of Confirmation in Relation to Baptism*.[1] In this, provoked by the discussions surrounding the recent publication of an official report on confirmation,[2] he again put forward an opinion he had defended in 1936, which had earlier found support among some

[1] Dacre Press, Westminster.
[2] *Confirmation Today. Report of the Joint Committees of the Convocations of Canterbury and York*, London (1944).

nineteenth-century Anglican theologians. It was that in Christian antiquity the various actions of initiation formed a unique rite of baptism: "baptism of water and the Spirit". In this one rite it was not the water but the "seal" that gave the Spirit. According to the ancient conception, the baptism by water was but a preliminary; it was baptism in the Spirit that had the positive effect of sealing the Christian for eternity. Unfortunately the West attributed the effects of both baptism of water and baptism of the Spirit to baptism by water. Western theology has wrongly attributed the effect of the more important rite to the rite that was only a preliminary. In other words, Dix stresses confirmation to the detriment of baptism. He allows to baptism itself only the negative effect of purification and the remission of sins. The positive effects of the gift of the Holy Spirit and the inpouring of grace belong exclusively to the second part of Christian initiation.

The view of Dix was attacked by Professor Lampe in his book, *The Seal of the Spirit*.[1] For him the Seal of the Spirit is given exclusively by baptism of water. He brings out the positive nature of baptism, but goes to the other extreme

---

[1] *The Seal of the Spirit: A Study in the Doctrine of Baptism and Confirmation in the New Testament and the Fathers*, by G. W. H. Lampe. London (1951).

and minimizes the meaning of confirmation. Its distinctive rites of anointing and laying on of hands are later developments and show a breaking-up of the primitive baptismal ritual. He denies that any special sacramental gift is given in confirmation, though it may be taken as symbolizing a commission to the apostolate.

It is not to my purpose to pursue the Anglican controversy further. I have mentioned it to illustrate the difficulty of an either-or approach to the problem. We must refuse to choose between the alternatives as presented in the dilemma, the Holy Spirit is given either in baptism or in confirmation. The answer to the problem lies in a both-and. Baptism by water is sufficient of itself for salvation; this is the constant tradition of the Church. Consequently its effect cannot be merely negative. It must give the life of grace as well as the remission of sins. But there is no life of grace without the Holy Spirit. On the other hand, confirmation completes baptism, and as a sacrament has its special grace to contribute. This is not just an increase of the baptismal grace but a perfective grace that finishes a work otherwise incomplete. Tradition calls this perfective grace the gift of the Spirit. So, both baptism and confirmation in their respective ways give the Holy Spirit. What distinguishes the gift of the Spirit in confirmation from that in baptism?

Two of the attempts by Catholic theologians to answer this question have remained without much support. At the end of the nineteenth century Johann Oswald argued for a distinction between a merely dynamic presence of the Holy Spirit and the formal, substantial presence of indwelling. A merely dynamic presence was given by baptism, the indwelling by confirmation. Two decades later, in 1920, Karl Adam expressed his agreement with this opinion. A different distinction was made by the Jesuit, Johann Umberg. He maintained that, although the indwelling of the Holy Spirit is given in baptism, the seven gifts of the Spirit are not given until confirmation.[1]

The reasons for the rejection of these views belong to the theology of grace. Theologians generally regard sanctifying grace and the indwelling of the Holy Spirit as inseparably connected, at least in the Christian economy of grace. There is no remission of sins without sanctifying grace; there is no sanctifying grace

[1] See his article "Confirmatione baptismus 'perficitur'", in *Ephemerides Theologicae Lovanienses*, 1 (1924), pp. 505–17, especially pp. 515–17. I owe the information about the opinion of Oswald and Adam to this article.

without the indwelling of the Spirit; therefore
baptism in remitting sins gives the indwelling
of the Spirit. Furthermore, the seven gifts of the
Holy Spirit are generally regarded as bound up
with the state of grace, as part of the equipment,
as it were, needed by the person to live the life
of grace. I am not suggesting that there is
nothing to be said for the unusual views I have
mentioned. But they do cause difficulty in the
theology of grace. Is it necessary to do this in
explaining confirmation? It does not seem so.
It is possible to seek the solution to the problem
of confirmation in another direction.

What is proper to confirmation is not the
coming of the Holy Spirit to dwell within us nor
the bestowal of the seven gifts. The Holy Spirit
comes to the baptized, dwells within them and
gives them his gifts. But there is a further coming in confirmation and a special increase in his
gifts. It is easy to be misled here by the inade-
quacy of language. The Holy Spirit does not
come by moving from one place to another, from
an imaginary heaven to a space within us. The
Spirit comes by establishing or strengthening a
relation with us, and all the change this involves
takes place on our side. The coming in confirmation has a purpose distinct from the coming in
baptism and therefore has different effects.
There is a sending of the Holy Spirit upon those

being baptized and a sending upon the same people when they are confirmed. But each of the two missions has its own purpose. The purpose of the mission in confirmation is so characteristic of the Holy Spirit, so pre-eminently his, that this sacrament is in a special way the sacrament of the Holy Spirit and its grace the special gift of the Holy Spirit.

The reason why the Holy Spirit comes in confirmation is to make the Christian a witness of Christ. Already members of Christ by baptism, Christians by confirmation become messengers of Christ and heralds of his Gospel. Now, a work ascribed in a special way to the Holy Spirit in the Bible is that of constituting a man as a prophet or spokesman of God and making him speak God's word and bear true testimony.

The Fathers explained confirmation by comparing it with Christ's anointing with the Spirit at his baptism in the Jordan and with the descent of the Spirit upon the Apostles at Pentecost. Christians are anointed with the Spirit as Christ was after his baptism. The first Christians received this anointing at Pentecost; confirmation is the Pentecost of each new member. These two traditional themes both lead to the same conclusion: Confirmation is the sacrament of prophets and martyrs or, to put it less dramatically, the sacrament making us witnesses of Christ.

The baptism of Jesus in the Jordan has already been considered. It marked the inauguration of his public ministry and was a solemn messianic anointing. This anointing was an anointing with the Spirit, and the Spirit came down upon Christ as he emerged from the water. True, as the Fathers observed, Christ was anointed at the moment of the Incarnation, since from the beginning of his life on earth Jesus was the Christ, which means the Anointed, and was indeed the only-begotten Son of God. But to show men that he was the Christ, he was publicly anointed again with the Spirit at the Jordan.

Christ was anointed with the Spirit for his mission of preaching and his work as Messiah. ("Messiah" is the Hebrew equivalent of "Christ" and means Anointed.) He himself declared the meaning of his anointing in the synagogue of Nazareth, using the words of Isaiah:

> Then he came to Nazareth, where he had been brought up; and he went into the synagogue there, as his custom was, on the sabbath day, and stood up to read. The book given to him was the book of the prophet Isaias; so he opened it, and found the place where the words ran: The Spirit of the Lord is upon me; he has anointed me, and sent me out to preach the gospel to the poor, to restore the broken-

hearted; to bid the prisoners go free, and the blind have sight; to set the oppressed at liberty, to proclaim a year when men may find acceptance with the Lord, a day of retribution. Then he shut the book, and gave it back to the attendant, and sat down. All those who were in the synagogue fixed their eyes on him, and thus he began speaking to them, This scripture which I have read in your hearing is today fulfilled. [Luke 4.16–21.]

We may take it that the anointing Christ refers to by applying the text of Isaiah to himself is the anointing that took place at his baptism. It was then, at the beginning of his public life, that he was solemnly anointed by the Spirit for his work of proclaiming the good news of salvation. Afterwards the Spirit led him into the wilderness to do battle with the devil, whose work he was to destroy by his miracles of healing and finally by his death and resurrection. The temptations over and the devil confounded, Jesus began to preach. As Luke puts it: "And Jesus came back to Galilee with the power of the Spirit upon him; word of him went round through all the neighbouring country, and he began to preach in their synagogues, so that his praise was on all men's lips." (Luke 4.14–15.) It is in the very next verse that Luke begins to describe the incident at Nazareth in the passage

I have quoted. There is thus a clear connection in Luke's account between the coming of the Spirit upon Christ at his baptism and the declaration of Christ at Nazareth.

We read often in the Old Testament how the Spirit came upon the Prophets and filled them with power for their difficult work as bearers of the message of God. Christ is the prophet of the New Testament, marked out for his mission by the Holy Spirit after the baptism by John.

It was a share in the prophetic mission of Christ which the first Christian community received on the day of Pentecost. The great occasion has already been described. Recall that in his first sermon Peter quoted these words of the prophet Joel: "In the last times, God says, I will pour out my spirit upon all mankind, and your sons and daughters will be prophets. ... I will pour out my spirit in those days upon my servants and handmaids, so that they will prophesy." (Acts 2.17–18; cf. Joel 2.28–9.) And Peter affirmed that this promise had been fulfilled. The coming of the Holy Spirit had made the first Christians prophets, and all who joined them were to be made prophets in their turn.

Prophets? Do Christians really become prophets? Is foretelling the future a regular adjunct of the Christian life? The answer to the last question is clearly No. But that question is due

to a crude though common misunderstanding of
"prophet". "A prophet" does not mean "someone
who foresees the future." Some of the prophets
in the Old Testament looked into the future because they had to tell men about the salvation
and Saviour to come. But the important thing
was always the message of God, not foretelling
the future. What "a prophet" really means is "a
man who is the herald of God", the messenger
of God, one who bears witness to the invisible
reality of God and tells men of his wonderful
works.

The first Christians became prophets at Pentecost as witnesses of Christ, spokesmen in his
cause, heralds of his message. It was for this that
Christ had promised them the Spirit: "The
Holy Spirit will come upon you, and you will
receive strength from him; you are to be my
witnesses in Jerusalem and throughout Judaea,
in Samaria, yes, and to the ends of the earth."
(Acts 1.8.) And the immediate effect of the
Spirit when he came on Pentecost Day was in
accord with this promise. At once Peter openly
proclaims Christ; the Church begins its mission
of bringing the message of Christ to all men, and
the gift of tongues was a symbol of the univer-
sality of that mission.

In brief, the Holy Spirit gave to the Christians
gathered together on Pentecost Day a share in

the mission of Christ the Prophet of the New Covenant. Their anointing with the Spirit corresponded to Christ's anointing at the Jordan. Its purpose was the same. They were anointed to proclaim the good news, but now the good news was that the death and resurrection of Christ had taken place, establishing the New Covenant. Of all this they were appointed witnesses.

The Greek word for witness is "martyr". To bear witness to Christ is to encounter opposition, persecution and often death. We call martyrs those who remain faithful witnesses even when it costs them their lives. But every true witness of Christ must be prepared for martyrdom, although not all are in fact called upon to show their faithfulness in this way. So, the first Christians, in becoming prophets or witnesses of Christ by the gift of the Spirit, were marked out for martyrdom by that same gift, and many of them did subsequently lay down their lives for Christ. Included in the gift of Pentecost was the call to martyrdom.

From the events of Pentecost emerged the Church as the new People of God, the messianic community. Immediately afterwards began the rites of baptism and confirmation. These two sacraments were used as the means whereby others were joined to the original fellowship and given a part in the gift of Pentecost. The role of confirmation in this handing on of Pentecost was to make the new members prophets or witnesses of Christ, with a share in his prophetic mission, the gift of the Spirit this presupposed and the call to martyrdom such a mission included.

If we now consider confirmation from this standpoint, the various statements about the sacrament fit together and become intelligible.

Confirmation completes baptism. Baptism incorporates us into Christ as his members; confirmation makes us his witnesses. The difference may be seen by contrasting confirmation with the anointing that immediately follows baptism. When the bishop consecrates the chrism on Maundy Thursday, he refers to the anointing with it of priests, kings, prophets and martyrs. The four offices may be divided, two apiece, between baptism and confirmation. At baptism Christians are anointed as priests and kings; by their baptism they are joined to Christ as Priest and King, made members of the priestly and kingly people of God, and this is symbolized by an anointing with chrism when they come from the water. Confirmation completes the initiation by giving the baptized a responsibility for the work of proclaiming Christ and anointing them as prophets and martyrs. It bestows a mission as witnesses upon them, and this gives them their full status as Christians.

It is this meaning of confirmation that probably explains why its rite originally consisted solely in the laying on of hands without a material anointing. Priests and kings were regularly anointed; prophets were not. The Spirit came down upon the Prophets and in that sense anointed them for their task, and at times this spiritual anointing was expressed outwardly by an anointing with oil; but the material anointing of prophets never had the same prominence as that of priests and kings. On the other hand, the apostolic Church chose in the laying on of hands an action of commissioning, indicating the giving of some task and the power to perform it—in this case, the task of bearing witness to Christ. Confirmation completes baptism by giving Christians their full responsibility in regard to the mission of the Church.

The anointing, however, was a valuable addition to the rite. The commissioning of a prophet is a work of the Holy Spirit. In the Creed of Constantinople used at Mass, the Holy Spirit is described with the phrase "qui locutus est per prophetas" ("who spoke by the prophets"). No one is a prophet except by a gift of the Holy Spirit; it is he who must be the source of our prophecy and witness. For that reason, confirmation is an anointing with the Spirit, aptly signified in the anointing with oil. The Spirit who came to us at baptism now comes upon us with fresh power and sends us forth as witnesses of Christ.

An ancient feature of the confirmation rite is the solemn invocation of the Spirit and his gifts. The function of the seven gifts of the Holy Spirit takes on a new importance in the confirmed. These gifts are permanent qualities within the Christian, making him sensitive to the action of the Spirit. We can think of how the texture and quality of a photographic film make it sensitive to light. Or, to use another example, the gifts form a sail which catches the movement and force coming from the Holy Spirit. By the gifts, then, we are made ready to receive the suggestions and promptings of the Spirit.

To count them precisely as seven is not important, but the list of seven usually given does describe seven ways in which the Spirit moves us and acts upon us. In four ways he enlightens the mind and in three ways he strengthens the will. He enlightens the mind with wisdom, understanding, knowledge and counsel. Wisdom is a taste for the things of God and an insight into them that comes from love. Understanding is a grasp of the truths of faith. Knowledge is a right appreciation of created things. Counsel is a sound judgement in practical matters concerning the Christian life. He strengthens the will with fortitude, piety and the fear of the Lord. Fortitude is spiritual courage when faced with difficulties. Piety draws us to God as our loving Father. Fear is a childlike reverence that makes us avoid displeasing him. Thus by his gifts the Spirit gives the Christian the knowledge and love needed to bear witness to Christ and guides and helps him in doing so.

Confirmation, then, is the Pentecost for each Christian. Like Pentecost for the first Christians, it is the coming of the Holy Spirit in power and a sharing in Christ's own anointing as Messiah and Prophet. True, we shall look in vain for the phenomena of Pentecost: the tongues of fire, the wind and the gift of tongues. But these were not the important factors in the event. They were given at the first Pentecost to mark the opening of the Church's work and attract the attention of men. But the interior gifts of the Spirit are still found. They are given with different signs. Instead of the tongues of fire, the wind and strange languages, we have the oil, the laying on of hands and the sign of the cross. Not so spectacular but just as powerful.

To become a witness of Christ by the gift of the Spirit is to assume an adult responsibility in the Church. Confirmation is the sacrament of Christian maturity; it makes us adult Christians. The difference between the child and the adult lies in the social responsibility of the adult. An adult does not live for himself alone; he works at the common task. He exercises a responsibility for others. Confirmation makes us Christian adults by appointing us as witnesses with the responsibility of bringing others into contact with Christ and his message.

In doing this confirmation gives us a permanent status in the Church. This sacrament confers a character and can be received only once. This means that it is concerned with our status and function within the organized body of the Church. Each character gives a particular place in the sacramental structure of the Church, with the functions and powers that go with it. The character of confirmation permanently consecrates us as witnesses, with the function and power of giving testimony to Christ and Christian realities through the activities that belong to a fully responsible member of the Christian community. Such activities will concern both life within the community itself and the impact of the community on the world.

This permanent consecration as witnesses is a further configuration to Christ as Priest. It has been said previously that all the characters are configurations to Christ the Priest and appoint the person to a place in the public worship of the Church. The baptismal character makes us members of the worshipping community. The character of confirmation completes this by giving to our membership and consequently to our worship its social and apostolic dimension. The liturgy of the Church is the centre where its mission to the world is constantly renewed. It is the confirmed who are able to exploit its full meaning and power. To this must be added that the prophetic mission of Christ is an aspect of his priesthood when this is adequately viewed. Priesthood in the Christian economy is concerned not only with sacrifice and sacrament but also with the word of God. This is so with Christ; it is so with the priesthood of his ministers, for preaching is a priestly function; it is so, too, with the common priesthood of all the faithful. Their function with regard to the word is given them by confirmation. That does not mean that they are preachers. The sacrament of holy order makes preachers and establishes authoritative teachers, the bishops, in the Church. But the witness of the Church is not confined to preaching and authoritative teaching; there is also the indispensable, multiple, ordinary witness of confirmed Christians. This is their share in the priesthood of the word. The divine endowment they receive in confirmation suffices to empower them for their general responsibilities. The confirmed, says St. Thomas, publicly profess the faith of Christ *quasi ex officio*.[1] But this endowment, the character, also renders the confirmed person an apt subject to receive from the bishop some part in the official teaching work of the Church—for example, by special authorization as a diocesan catechist.

This account of confirmation makes it easy to understand why confirmation has been extolled in recent years as the sacrament of Catholic Action. The activities of the organized lay apostolate are an admirable way of carrying out the responsibilities given in confirmation. And lay apostles working in the organized movements can call upon the grace of this sacrament. But it would be wrong to limit the meaning of this sacrament and the role of the confirmed to the sphere of Catholic Action. That would be an impoverishment and a distortion.

Many will be surprised that I have said nothing so far about confirmation as a sacrament of strength. Impressed on our minds is the catechism answer to the effect that confirmation makes us "strong and perfect Christians and soldiers of Jesus Christ". Now, the understanding of confirmation as the sacrament giving strength and courage for the Christian fight has had a bad press in recent years. There are several reasons

[1] *Summa Theologiae*, III, q. 72, a. 5, ad 2.

for this. The *locus classicus* for the idea in the Middle Ages was one the False Decretals, and a "decretal" attributed to a non-existent Pope Melchiades to boot. Next, the famous slap on the cheek given by the bishop after the anointing and interpreted as a symbol of blows we must be prepared to endure for Christ is a thirteenth-century allegorizing of the ancient kiss of peace. It does not provide a valid liturgical argument for confirmation as a sacrament of valiant combat. Further, the statement that confirmation makes us soldiers of Jesus Christ is misleading and can easily be understood in a way that is untraditional. Traditionally, it is baptism that enrols us in the army of Jesus Christ. The Liturgy makes this clear, particularly in the rite of renouncing Satan, which is followed in the East by a rite expressing adherence to Christ. The idea is that the baptized pass from the ranks of Satan to the ranks of Christ. Baptism marks the opening of our warfare with Satan, and this is the meaning of the exorcisms and the pre-baptismal anointing. Finally, confirmation is wrongly seen as the sacrament of our personal struggle with sin. The sacraments that provide the help to overcome sin after baptism are the Eucharist and penance. The presentation of confirmation as a means of coping with the moral difficulties of adolescence is a woeful twisting of its meaning. Confirmation is a sacrament received once only, for the bestowal of a status within the Church and a responsibility for its mission.

For these reasons there has been a reaction against the common view of confirmation as a strengthening to make us good soldiers of Christ. Now, while it is true that the average current account of confirmation is poor and narrow, leaving out important aspects of its meaning, to reject the idea of the sacrament of strength completely is an error. A long line of texts, from the Fathers onwards, presents this sacrament as giving courage and strength to the Christian and preparing him to do battle for Christ. But the context of the theme is the mission of the confirmed as witnesses. They receive courage and strength to profess the Faith and bear testimony to Christ. They do combat for the Faith, even, if necessary, to martyrdom. As late as the fifteenth century, the Council of Florence expressed it in this way:

> The effect of this sacrament is that a Christian may courageously confess the name of Christ, because in this sacrament the Holy Spirit is given for strength just as he was given to the Apostles on Pentecost. And therefore, the one to be confirmed is anointed on the forehead, where shame shows itself, lest he be ashamed to confess the name of Christ and especially his

cross which was, indeed, according to the
Apostle, a stumbling-block to the Jews and to
the Gentiles foolishness. And for this reason
the recipient is signed with the sign of the
cross.[1]

In brief, there is nothing wrong with seeing confirmation as a sacrament giving us strength to
be brave soldiers of Christ, provided that this is
explained in accord with the fundamental meaning of the sacrament.[2]

Confirmation completes the making of a
Christian, but it does so only by leading him to
the Eucharist and preparing him for it. Admittedly, all the baptized may already go to Mass
and, if of age, receive Holy Communion, but
confirmation, as we have seen, enables us to take
part in a new way. We are called by our confirmation to work with Christ for the salvation of men.
But the power of Christ to save comes from his
sacrifice on the Cross, and nothing can be done
except through the Cross to bring men salvation.
So, we must meet Christ in his sacrifice if we
want our witness to him to be filled with his

[1] Cf. Denzinger, 697. The English translation is from
The Church Teaches, St. Louis (1955), no. 707.

[2] For an account of recent discussions, see T. Camelot,
O.P., "Sur la théologie de la confirmation", in *Revue
des sciences philosophiques et théologiques*, 38 (1954),
pp. 637–57.

power and penetrated with his Spirit. That sacrifice is present for us in the Mass, and we join in it fully by Holy Communion.

Therefore, just as the Eucharist is the centre of the life of any baptized Christian and the source of his strength, so too it is the centre of the lives of all who are complete Christians and the source of their power as prophets and witnesses of Christ. The initiation of a Christian reaches its achievement in the Eucharist.